PAUL

A Man of Grace and Grit

INSIGHT FOR LIVING BIBLE STUDY GUIDE

From the Bible-teaching ministry of

CHARLES R. SWINDOLL

INSIGHT *for* LIVING

Insight for Living's Bible teacher, Chuck Swindoll, has devoted his life to the clear, practical application of God's Word and His grace. A pastor at heart, Chuck has served as senior pastor to congregations in Texas, Massachusetts, and California. He currently leads Stonebriar Community Church in Frisco, Texas, but Chuck's listening audience extends far beyond a local church body. As a leading program in Christian broadcasting, *Insight for Living* airs in major Christian radio markets, through more than 2,100 outlets worldwide, in 16 languages, and to a growing webcast audience. Chuck's extensive writing ministry has also served the body of Christ worldwide, and his leadership as president and now chancellor of Dallas Theological Seminary has helped prepare and equip a new generation for ministry. Chuck and Cynthia, his partner in life and ministry, have four grown children and ten grandchildren.

Based on the outlines and transcripts of Charles R. Swindoll's sermons, charts, the study guide text was developed and written by the creative ministries department of Insight for Living.

Editor in Chief:
Cynthia Swindoll

Editor:
Amy LaFuria

Study Guide Writers:
Marla Alupoaicei
Suzanne Keffer
Brian Goins
Mark Tobey

Rights and Permissions:
The Meredith Agency

Typesetter:
Bob Haskins

Unless otherwise identified, all Scripture references are from the *New American Standard Bible* © The Lockman Foundation 1960, 1962, 1963, 1968, 1971, 1972, 1973, 1975, 1977, 1995. Used by permission. Scripture taken from the *Holy Bible*, New International Version, Copyright © 1973, 1978, 1984 International Bible Society, used by permission of Zondervan Bible Publishers [NIV]. Scripture quotations from *The Message* © 1993, 1994, 1995 by Eugene H. Peterson used by permission of Nav Press Publishing Group.

Material from *The Apostle: A Life of Paul* © 1985 by John Pollock used by permission of Cook Communications Ministries. May not be further reproduced. All rights reserved.

An effort has been made to locate sources and obtain permission where necessary for the quotations used in this book. In the event of any unintentional omission, a modification will gladly be incorporated in future printings.

ISBN: 1-57972-447-7
Cover design: Shawn Sturm. Adapted from the hardback cover design by David Carlson Design
Cover image: David Bowers
Printed in the United States of America

CONTENTS

INTRODUCTION

Scholars, authors, and painters often depict the apostle Paul as a solemn individual who spent all his time piously meditating over his books. Some portraits even include a halo glowing softly just above Paul's head. But our desire is to dispel that image and give you an up-close-and-personal look at the real apostle Paul.

The man was neither tall nor handsome. He didn't possess powerful oratory skills. He struggled with a physical ailment that was so severe that he called it his "thorn in the flesh." He faced rejection by his family and friends. He was beaten and left near death by those with whom he communicated the Gospel. Paul was what I like to call "a man of grace and grit." He modeled an active, authentic faith. What he lacked in physical stature and eloquence, he made up for in passion and determination to make the message of Jesus Christ known. Paul possessed a fire for God that no one could quench.

The man from ancient Tarsus knew what it was like to grow up under a law that no one could fully keep. He understood the need for something more—salvation through Christ the Lord for all who believe. The better we understand the apostle's past, the events surrounding his conversion, and his effective ministry, the better we'll understand his incredible gratitude for grace.

As we shall see, Paul learned vital lessons and experienced more than a few interesting adventures on his spiritual pilgrimage. We'll also discover some life-changing insights as we follow in the great apostle's footsteps.

Join us now as we set out to dispel the erroneous myths surrounding this man of God who was no cloistered saint tucked away in a dusty study. Get ready to meet the real Paul—a man of grace and grit. And be prepared for a few surprises along the way!

Chuck Swindoll

Charles R. Swindoll

PUTTING TRUTH INTO ACTION

K nowledge apart from application falls short of God's desire for His children. He wants us to apply what we learn so that we will change and grow. This Bible study guide was prepared with these goals in mind. As you go through the following pages, we hope your desire to discover biblical truth will grow as your understanding of God's Word increases and that you will be encouraged to apply what you've learned.

To assist you in your study, we've included a section called *Living Insights* at the end of each lesson. These exercises will challenge you to study further and to think of specific ways to put your discoveries into action.

On occasion a lesson is followed by a ✎ **Digging Deeper** section, which gives you additional information and resources to probe further into issues raised in that lesson.

We've also added ✿**Questions for Group Discussion,** which are formulated to get your group talking and sharing ideas about the key issues in each lesson.

There are many ways to use this guide—in personal devotions, group studies, discussions with friends and family, and Sunday School classes. And, of course, it's an ideal study aid when you're listening to its corresponding *Insight for Living* radio series.

To benefit most from this Bible study guide, we encourage you to consider it a spiritual journal. That's why we've included space in the **Living Insights** for recording your thoughts and discoveries. We hope you'll return to those sections often for review and encouragement as you continue to grow in your walk with Christ.

Insight for Living

PAUL

A Man of Grace and Grit

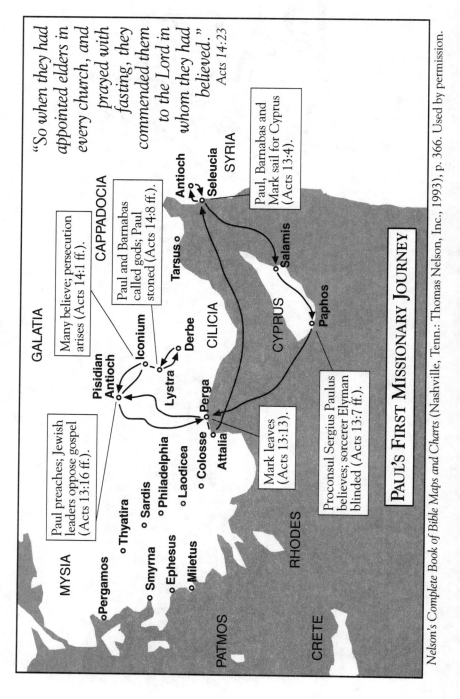

"So when they had appointed elders in every church, and prayed with fasting, they commended them to the Lord in whom they had believed."
Acts 14:23

Paul, Barnabas and Mark sail for Cyprus (Acts 13:4).

Many believe; persecution arises (Acts 14:1 ff.).

Paul and Barnabas called gods; Paul stoned (Acts 14:8 ff.).

Paul preaches; Jewish leaders oppose gospel (Acts 13:16 ff.).

Mark leaves (Acts 13:13).

Proconsul Sergius Paulus believes; sorcerer Elyman blinded (Acts 13:7 ff.).

PAUL'S FIRST MISSIONARY JOURNEY

GALATIA

CAPPADOCIA

MYSIA

Pergamos

Thyatira

Smyrna

Sardis

Philadelphia

Ephesus

Laodicea

Miletus

Colosse

Pisidian Antioch

Iconium

Lystra

Derbe

Tarsus

Perga

Attalia

CILICIA

RHODES

PATMOS

CRETE

CYPRUS

Paphos

Salamis

Antioch

Seleucia

SYRIA

Nelson's Complete Book of Bible Maps and Charts (Nashville, Tenn.: Thomas Nelson, Inc., 1993), p. 366. Used by permission.

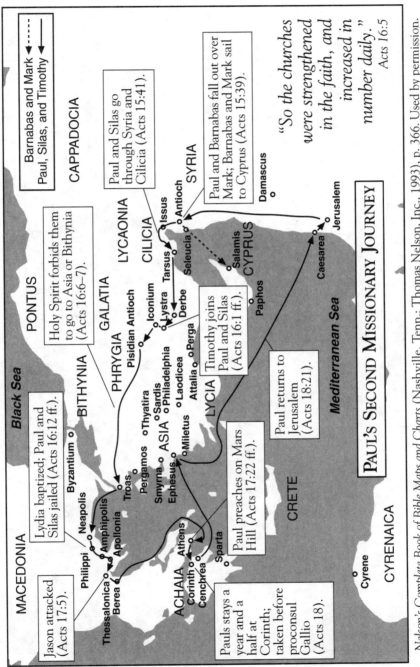

PAUL'S SECOND MISSIONARY JOURNEY

Barnabas and Mark ▸▸▸▸▸▸
Paul, Silas, and Timothy ▬▶

Paul and Silas go through Syria and Cilicia (Acts 15:41).

Holy Spirit forbids them to go to Asia or Bithynia (Acts 16:6–7).

Paul and Barnabas fall out over Mark; Barnabas and Mark sail to Cyprus (Acts 15:39).

Lydia baptized; Paul and Silas jailed (Acts 16:12 ff.).

Timothy joins Paul and Silas (Acts 16:1 ff.).

Paul returns to Jerusalem (Acts 18:21).

Jason attacked (Acts 17:5).

Paul preaches on Mars Hill (Acts 17:22 ff.).

Pauls stays a year and a half at Corinth; taken before proconsul Gallio (Acts 18).

"So the churches were strengthened in the faith, and increased in number daily."
Acts 16:5

CAPPADOCIA

PONTUS

BITHYNIA

GALATIA

PHRYGIA

LYCAONIA

CILICIA

SYRIA

ASIA

LYCIA

MACEDONIA

ACHAIA

CRETE

CYRENAICA

Black Sea

Mediterranean Sea

Byzantium
Neapolis
Philippi
Amphipolis
Apollonia
Thessalonica
Berea
Athens
Corinth
Cenchrea
Sparta
Troas
Pergamos
Thyatira
Smyrna
Sardis
Philadelphia
Ephesus
Laodicea
Attalia
Miletus
Perga
Pisidian Antioch
Iconium
Lystra
Derbe
Tarsus
Issus
Antioch
Seleucia
Salamis
Paphos
CYPRUS
Damascus
Caesarea
Jerusalem
Cyrene

Nelson's Complete Book of Bible Maps and Charts (Nashville, Tenn.: Thomas Nelson, Inc., 1993), p. 366. Used by permission.

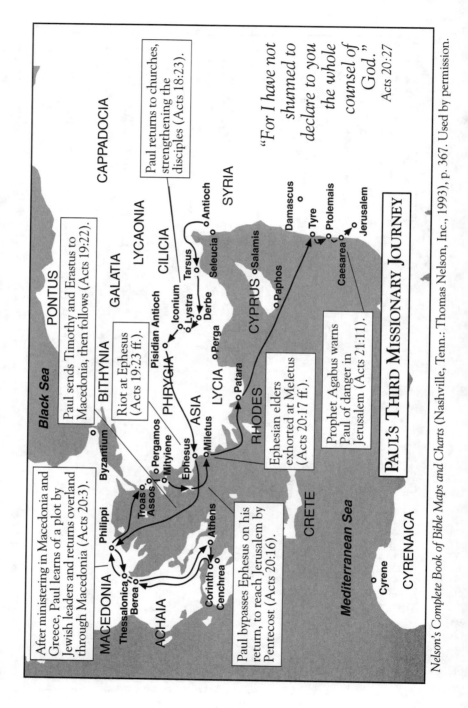

PAUL'S THIRD MISSIONARY JOURNEY

Black Sea

Mediterranean Sea

PONTUS

CAPPADOCIA

BITHYNIA

GALATIA

LYCAONIA

PHRYGIA

ASIA

CILICIA

LYCIA

RHODES

CYPRUS

SYRIA

CRETE

CYRENAICA

MACEDONIA

ACHAIA

Byzantium

Philippi

Thessalonica

Berea

Troas

Assos

Mitylene

Pergamos

Ephesus

Miletus

Patara

Athens

Corinth

Cenchrea

Perga

Pisidian Antioch

Iconium

Lystra

Derbe

Tarsus

Antioch

Seleucia

Salamis

Paphos

Damascus

Tyre

Ptolemais

Caesarea

Jerusalem

Cyrene

After ministering in Macedonia and Greece, Paul learns of a plot by Jewish leaders and returns overland through Macedonia (Acts 20:3).

Paul sends Timothy and Erastus to Macedonia, then follows (Acts 19:22).

Riot at Ephesus (Acts 19:23 ff.).

Paul returns to churches, strengthening the disciples (Acts 18:23).

Ephesian elders exhorted at Meletus (Acts 20:17 ff.).

Prophet Agabus warns Paul of danger in Jerusalem (Acts 21:11).

Paul bypasses Ephesus on his return, to reach Jerusalem by Pentecost (Acts 20:16).

"For I have not shunned to declare to you the whole counsel of God."
Acts 20:27

Nelson's Complete Book of Bible Maps and Charts (Nashville, Tenn.: Thomas Nelson, Inc., 1993), p. 367. Used by permission.

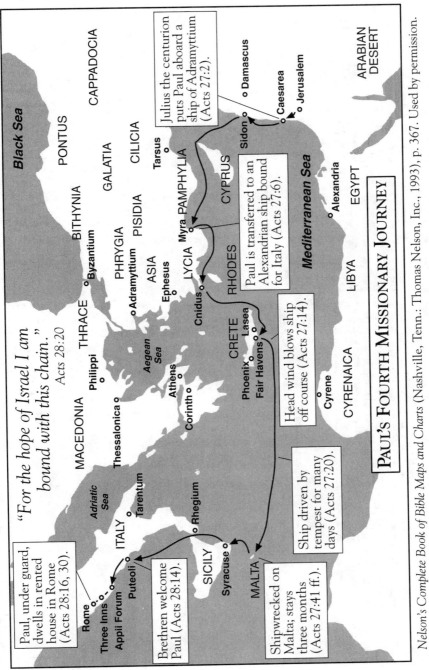

PAUL'S FOURTH MISSIONARY JOURNEY

"For the hope of Israel I am bound with this chain."
Acts 28:20

Julius the centurion puts Paul aboard a ship of Adramyttium (Acts 27:2).

Paul is transferred to an Alexandrian ship bound for Italy (Acts 27:6).

Head wind blows ship off course (Acts 27:14).

Ship driven by tempest for many days (Acts 27:20).

Shipwrecked on Malta; stays three months (Acts 27:41 ff.).

Brethren welcome Paul (Acts 28:14).

Paul, under guard, dwells in rented house in Rome (Acts 28:16, 30).

Nelson's Complete Book of Bible Maps and Charts (Nashville, Tenn.: Thomas Nelson, Inc., 1993), p. 367. Used by permission.

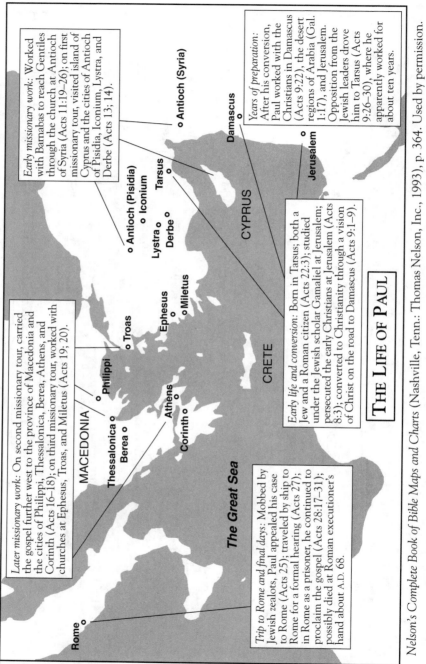

THE LIFE OF PAUL

Early missionary work: Worked with Barnabas to reach Gentiles through the church at Antioch of Syria (Acts 11:19–26); on first missionary tour, visited island of Cyprus and the cities of Antioch of Pisidia, Iconium, Lystra, and Derbe (Acts 13; 14).

Years of preparation: After his conversion, Paul worked with the Christians in Damascus (Acts 9:22), the desert regions of Arabia (Gal. 1:17), and Jerusalem. Opposition from the Jewish leaders drove him to Tarsus (Acts 9:26–30), where he apparently worked for about ten years.

Later missionary work: On second missionary tour, carried the gospel further west to the province of Macedonia and the cities of Philippi, Thessalonica, Berea, Athens, and Corinth (Acts 16–18); on third missionary tour, worked with churches at Ephesus, Troas, and Miletus (Acts 19; 20).

Early life and conversion: Born in Tarsus; both a Jew and a Roman citizen (Acts 22:3); studied under the Jewish scholar Gamaliel at Jerusalem; persecuted the early Christians at Jerusalem (Acts 8:3); converted to Christianity through a vision of Christ on the road to Damascus (Acts 9:1–9).

Trip to Rome and final days: Mobbed by Jewish zealots, Paul appealed his case to Rome (Acts 25); traveled by ship to Rome for a formal hearing (Acts 27); in Rome as a prisoner, he continued to proclaim the gospel (Acts 28:17–31); possibly died at Roman executioner's hand about A.D. 68.

Antioch (Syria)

Damascus

Jerusalem

CYPRUS

Tarsus

Antioch (Pisidia)

Iconium

Lystra

Derbe

Ephesus

Miletus

Troas

MACEDONIA

Philippi

Thessalonica

Berea

Athens

Corinth

CRETE

The Great Sea

Rome

Nelson's Complete Book of Bible Maps and Charts (Nashville, Tenn.: Thomas Nelson, Inc., 1993), p. 364. Used by permission.

Chapter 1

MAY I INTRODUCE TO YOU SAUL OF TARSUS
Acts 5:12–39; 7:54–8:3

Many heroes have unlikely beginnings.

Charles Lindbergh was one such individual who rose to the ranks of American heroes out of virtual obscurity. Raised in a broken family, Lindbergh grew up a recluse, choosing to wander the dense woods near his childhood home rather than submit to the rigors of academics. Though strikingly handsome, he had an awkward manner when dealing with people. Most surprisingly, his aviation career began as a sideshow. He earned his keep barnstorming sleepy Midwestern towns, wowing small crowds of locals in his airplane.

Yet, from the dust of those humble beginnings, Charles Lindbergh climbed to altitudes of staggering success. In 1927 he completed the world's first ever transatlantic flight by a pilot, joining two continents divided by sea. In a gala event celebrating Lindbergh's heroic achievement, one American statesman proclaimed, "We measure heroes as we do ships, by their displacement. Charles Lindbergh displaced everything." [1]

Lindbergh's triumph illustrates the limitless power of an ordinary life propelled by an extraordinary vision. With sheer grit and undaunted courage, this unlikely flyboy from Minnesota altered aviation history.

---

1. A. Scott Berg, *Lindbergh* (New York, N.Y.: G. P. Putnam's Sons, Penguin Putnam, 1998), p. 159.

The apostle Paul, too, displaced everything. No other disciple in the history of Christianity had such an impact on the development of the church. Paul's story illustrates the power of a solitary life surrendered to a singular, driving vision—the reality of the risen Christ.

Yet, like Lindbergh, Paul's life was full of surprises, not the least of which was his career before his encounter with Christ. As we embark on our study of Paul, we must brace ourselves for some shocking jolts along the way. Luke's straightforward account in the book of Acts detailing the apostle's rocky rise to heroism will challenge our preconceptions. We'll soon discover that our view of the missionary statesman from Tarsus may be incomplete. Most of us happily embrace Paul's magnificent career as the apostle of grace and peace. But few take time to consider his surprising past, stained with the blood of Christians.

A Career of Brutality

A scene from Acts 7 reflects Saul's hatred for Christ's followers. The scene's primary focus is on Stephen, a young, zealous follower of Christ who had just delivered a scathing rebuke against the Jewish leaders. As the self-righteous religious leaders listened to Stephen's words, their indignation blazed into fury:

> Now when they heard this, they were cut to the quick, and they began gnashing their teeth at him. But being full of the Holy Spirit, he gazed intently into heaven and saw the glory of God, and Jesus standing at the right hand of God; and he said, "Behold, I see the heavens opened up and the Son of Man standing at the right hand of God." But they cried out with a loud voice, and covered their ears and rushed at him with one impulse. (Acts 7:54–57)

In the midst of the raging mob stood a leading Pharisee named Saul (not yet called Paul). He watched approvingly as the young church leader met his violent end in the shadow of the city gates. He even guarded the robes of those who were stoning Stephen:

> When they had driven him out of the city, they began stoning him; and the witnesses laid aside their robes at the feet of a young man named Saul. They went on stoning Stephen as he called on the Lord

and said, "Lord Jesus, receive my spirit!" Then falling on his knees, he cried out with a loud voice, "Lord, do not hold this sin against them!" Having said this, he fell asleep. (vv. 58–60)

After Stephen's death, Saul lashed out against Christians with renewed energy. The beginning of Acts 8 records his zealous persecution of the church:

> Saul was in hearty agreement with putting him to death.
> And on that day a great persecution began against the church in Jerusalem, and they were all scattered throughout the regions of Judea and Samaria, except the apostles. Some devout men buried Stephen, and made loud lamentation over him. But Saul began ravaging the church, entering house after house, and dragging off men and women, he would put them in prison. (8:1–3)

One scholar comments on this period of intense religious persecution:

> In his speeches, Paul indicates that, blinded by zeal, he persecuted numerous people. When they were put to death, he gave his approval ([see Acts] 26:10). Hence his concurrence with Stephen's execution was only the beginning of a murderous career.
> . . . Saul flushed out the Christians and handed them over to the jailers.[2]

Is this our hero? A witness who condoned violence against believers and ravaged the church in the name of God? It's hard for us to imagine the gracious apostle we find in the later epistles taking part in such brutality. Yet Scripture does not flinch from the cruelty of his past.

Prepared to Persecute

How did Saul get to this point? What about his background, education, and upbringing? Let's take a closer look at Saul's past to see how it shaped his life.

2. Simon J. Kistemaker, *New Testament Commentary: Exposition of the Acts of the Apostles* (Grand Rapids, Mich.: Baker Book House, 1990), p. 289.

Saul's Sphere of Life

Saul was from the city of Tarsus, a bustling metropolis nestled near the Mediterranean Sea, in the shadow of the Taurus Mountains. The city prospered as a strategic trade hub of the Roman world. Paul later noted the status of his birthplace by saying, "I am a Jew of Tarsus in Cilicia, a citizen of no insignificant city" (21:39). Tarsus probably would have topped the list of "Best Places to Live" in the ancient world. Sophisticated and cosmopolitan, the city glittered like a diamond on the hand of a queen.

As a youth, Saul spent most of his days in a world of exacting religious observance, gaining a first-rate education. Influenced by his devout Jewish family, Saul mastered the Hebrew Scriptures, studied the Law at the feet of the leading teacher of his day, Gamaliel, in the influential school of Jerusalem, and rapidly ascended to a coveted seat as a member of the Sanhedrin.

Saul's passion for his religion soon collided head-on with the apostles' passion for Christ. Quite likely, he was numbered among the Jewish leaders who plotted to silence the apostles in Acts 5.

When Worlds Collide

In Acts 5, we find Jerusalem humming with extraordinary religious activity. The emboldened preaching of Christ's apostles drew thousands to embrace the Messiah. Through the power of the Holy Spirit, these men healed disease-ravaged bodies and offered hope to sin-sick souls:

> At the hands of the apostles many signs and wonders were taking place among the people; and they were all with one accord in Solomon's portico. But none of the rest dared to associate with them; however, the people held them in high esteem. And all the more believers in the Lord, multitudes of men and women, were constantly added to their number, to such an extent that they even carried the sick out into the streets and laid them on cots and pallets, so that when Peter came by at least his shadow might fall on any one of them. Also the people from the cities in the vicinity of Jerusalem were coming together, bringing people who were sick or afflicted with unclean spirits, and they were all being healed. (Acts 5:12–16)

4

The growing popularity of the apostles posed a dire threat to the religious leaders' insatiable appetite for power. To protect their rule, they agreed to take drastic measures:

> But the high priest rose up, along with all his associates (that is the sect of the Sadducees), and they were filled with jealousy. They laid hands on the apostles and put them in a public jail. (vv. 17–18)

Saul most likely took part in carrying out the high priest's directive. To him, a few nights in chains fell short of what the blasphemous infidels deserved. Saul and the others discovered, however, that no public jail could contain the powerful message of life these Spirit-filled men proclaimed:

> But during the night an angel of the Lord opened the gates of the prison, and taking [the apostles] out he said, "Go, stand and speak to the people in the temple the whole message of this Life." Upon hearing this, they entered into the temple about daybreak and began to teach. (vv. 19–21)

The Sadducees' initial attempt at "cultic cleansing" failed miserably. The apostles went right back to preaching, more emboldened than ever! When the report of the apostles' mysterious escape from prison reached the religious officials, they were, in Luke's words, "greatly perplexed" (v. 24). But they were not swayed from their plans, and once again, the apostles were brought to the Council (vv. 25–26).[3] The apostles' response to the next round of interrogations was remarkable:

> The high priest questioned them, saying, "We gave you strict orders not to continue teaching in this name, and yet, you have filled Jerusalem with your teaching and intend to bring this man's blood upon us." But Peter and the apostles answered, "We must obey God rather than men." (vv. 27–29)

---

3. The "Council" most likely refers to the Sanhedrin, the powerful ruling body of Jewish leaders headquartered in Jerusalem. It would have been composed of both present and former high priests, Pharisees, Sadducees, and scribes (the legal experts). One author notes that by the time of the early church, appointments to the Council were "no longer hereditary, but political, and ex-high priests with their close associates (such as the captain of the Temple) made up the 'rulers' (John 7:26; Acts 4:5–8, and so forth)." See J. D. Douglas and others, eds., *New Bible Dictionary*, 2d ed. (Downers Grove, Ill.: InterVarsity Press, 1982), pp. 1070–72.

Saul heard that speech, just as he would hear Stephen's, and observed a triumphant resolve and bold conviction in these apostles. Perhaps Peter's defense gnawed at Saul's soul as the burly preacher from Galilee warmed to his point:

> "The God of our fathers raised up Jesus, whom you had put to death by hanging Him on a cross. He is the one whom God exalted to His right hand as a Prince and a Savior, to grant repentance to Israel, and forgiveness of sins. And we are witnesses of these things; and so is the Holy Spirit, whom God has given to those who obey Him." (vv. 30–32)

With that, the whole lot of religious leaders grew furious. The insidious frustration they harbored against this band of unruly infidels erupted into a murderous rage. Yet from within their religious ranks arose someone to give the apostles aid. Surprisingly, it was Gamaliel, Saul's own teacher:

> But when they heard this, they were cut to the quick and intended to kill them. But a Pharisee named Gamaliel, a teacher of the Law, respected by all the people, stood up in the Council and gave orders to put the men outside for a short time. (vv. 33–34)

Saul must have stood stunned as he watched his seasoned mentor calmly take control of the chaotic scene:

> And [Gamaliel] said to them, "Men of Israel, take care what you propose to do with these men. For some time ago Theudas rose up, claiming to be somebody, and a group of about four hundred men joined up with him. But he was killed, and all who followed him were dispersed and came to nothing. After this man, Judas of Galilee rose up in the days of the census and drew away some people after him; he too perished, and all those who followed him were scattered. So in the present case, I say to you, stay away from these men and let them alone, for if this plan or action is of men, it will be overthrown; but if it is of God, you will not be able to overthrow them; or else you may even be found fighting against God." (vv. 35–39)

No doubt you could have heard a pin drop as the frenzied lot of angry judges blinked and stared in disbelief. A calmer head had prevailed. Following a stern warning against preaching the Gospel, the apostles were flogged and then set free. Luke reports that they went straight back to "teaching and preaching Jesus as the Christ" (v. 42)!

Meanwhile, Saul must have fumed as he watched the apostles get off scot-free. In his zeal for his religion, Saul resolved to rid Jerusalem and the surrounding regions of the "Messiah menace" forever.

Reflections on a Blood-Stained Past

How could such a high-impact New Testament apostle and writer emerge from a man of such spiritual blindness and physical brutality? The answer: amazing grace! It was God's grace alone that transformed Saul, a bitter enemy of the Gospel, into Paul, an ambassador of Jesus Christ. As we reflect on this stormy beginning to such a magnificent life, three principles emerge that help put matters in perspective.

First, *no matter how we appear to others, everyone has a dark side.* That includes you and me. Human nature at its core is turned away from God, the source and embodiment of all that is good. That's why it should come as no surprise to us when an individual so revered and respected as the apostle Paul had a checkered past. We all do to some extent. Paul wrote, "For all have sinned and fall short of the glory of God" (Rom. 3:23). That little word *all* packs a powerful theological punch. *All* of us have a past marred by sin.

Second, *regardless of what you have done, you are not beyond hope.* That's the Good News of the Gospel! We are not without hope. Neither was Saul. When the Lord saved him on the Damascus road (a story we will visit in detail in the next chapter), He didn't place him on probation. Others did, but God didn't. There's nothing in your past beyond the reach of God's warm embrace in Christ. His grace reaches to the lowest valley, no matter where you've been.

And third, *even though your past is soiled, you can find a new beginning with God.* Now isn't that great news? The point is, it's never too late to start doing what's right. You can begin again because of God's grace. Like Saul, you are not chained to your sinful past. The Lord's grace gives you wings to leave the past behind and soar into a brand-new tomorrow!

7

Living Insights

Aren't you glad that God, in His grace, doesn't sigh in exasperation and give up on His fallen people? Instead, He lovingly embraces us and lifts us out of the pit of despair.

Do you know the comfort and reassurance of His embrace? Or are there issues from your past that still plague you at times? If so, what steps can you take to work through them?

_____

_____

_____

_____

_____

God has been with you in every step you have taken, whether you were aware of it or not. Take a moment now to pray, asking the Lord to remind you of how you have seen His grace in your life. Write down what He brings to mind.

_____

_____

_____

_____

How have you shared, or how will you share, your hope with others?

_____

_____

_____

_____

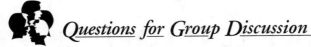 ## Questions for Group Discussion

1. Have you been surprised by some of the things you have learned from this chapter about Saul's background and behavior? If so, what?

2. What character traits did Saul display as he zealously persecuted Christians in his early life? How did these traits serve him in his later ministry?

3. Name a time when you saw God work in a miraculous way in someone's life. What occurred, and how did it affect your faith?

4. What have you learned about evangelism from the apostles' example in this chapter? How does this encourage you to share your faith with others?

Chapter 2

THE VIOLENT CAPTURE OF A REBEL WILL
Acts 9:1–9

The captain of the ship looked into the dark night and saw faint lights in the distance. Immediately he told his signalman to send a message: "Alter your course 10 degrees south."

Promptly a return message was received: "Alter your course 10 degrees north."

The captain was angered; his command had been ignored. So he sent a second message: "Alter your course 10 degrees south—I am the captain!"

Soon another message was received: "Alter your course 10 degrees north—I am seaman third class Jones."

Immediately the captain sent a third message, knowing the fear it would evoke: "Alter your course 10 degrees south—I am a battleship!"

Then the reply came: "Alter your course 10 degrees north—I am a lighthouse."[1]

What does it take to alter the course of an enormous battleship? It takes a convincing message that continuing on its current course will mean certain destruction. Only then does reality hit that the ship is headed in the wrong direction.

That's precisely what happened to Saul on the Damascus road. Driven by battleship-sized pride and steel determination, he was on a collision course with his eternal destiny when he suddenly came face-to-face with the Light of the World. Only then did he realize that he had been headed in the wrong direction.

Let's take a closer look at his dramatic conversion and see how the risen Christ captured Saul's rebel will and transformed him into an instrument of grace.

---

1. *Leadership* magazine, Spring 1983, as quoted by Charles R. Swindoll in *The Tale of the Tardy Oxcart and 1,501 Other Stories* (Nashville, Tenn.: Word Publishing, 1998), pp. 539–40.

From a Violent Rebel to a Humbled Servant

The book of Acts and other passages in the New Testament contain the apostle Paul's description of his sinful life prior to his encounter with Jesus on the Damascus road. The following passages represent a brief survey of Paul's remarkable words:

> "I am a Jew, born in Tarsus of Cilicia, but brought up in this city, educated under Gamaliel, strictly according to the law of our fathers, being zealous for God just as you all are today. I persecuted this Way to the death, binding and putting both men and women into prisons, as also the high priest and all the Council of the elders can testify. From them I also received letters to the brethren, and started off for Damascus in order to bring even those who were there to Jerusalem as prisoners to be punished." (Acts 22:3–5)

> "So then, I thought to myself that I had to do many things hostile to the name of Jesus of Nazareth. And this is just what I did in Jerusalem; not only did I lock up many of the saints in prisons, having received authority from the chief priests, but also when they were being put to death I cast my vote against them. And as I punished them often in all the synagogues, I tried to force them to blaspheme; and being furiously enraged at them, I kept pursuing them even to foreign cities." (Acts 26:9–11)

> For you have heard of my former manner of life in Judaism, how I used to persecute the church of God beyond measure and tried to destroy it; and I was advancing in Judaism beyond many of my contemporaries among my countrymen, being more extremely zealous for my ancestral traditions. (Gal. 1:13–14)

Paul resisted the temptation to sugarcoat his past. He laid it out plainly as he shared his testimony of God's grace in his life. He understood how far mercy had to reach to lift him out of the pit. As we will see next, Luke's stirring account in Acts 9 details the miraculous transformation that occurred when a blinding light from heaven opened the eyes of this future disciple's heart.

A Roadside Conversion

> Now Saul, still breathing threats and murder
> against the disciples of the Lord, went to the high
> priest, and asked for letters from him to the syna-
> gogues at Damascus, so that if he found any belong-
> ing to the Way, both men and women, he might
> bring them bound to Jerusalem. (Acts 9:1–2)

Following Stephen's violent murder, Saul's mission intensified
as he ravaged the church in Jerusalem, but that field of prey grew
thin. As one scholar notes, the zealous Pharisee's appetite for the
blood of Christians drove him to hunt in fresh territory:

> He was already a person of influence in Jerusalem,
> marked out as a leader by his intense and devouring
> enthusiasm, especially where something exceptional
> or dangerous had to be done. The stoning of
> Stephen, though stoning was permitted by the Jew-
> ish law in cases of exceptional and gross impiety,
> was dangerous to the perpetrators as being contrary
> to Roman law. This disgraceful act, and the even
> more disgraceful persecution which followed (more
> disgraceful because more cold-blooded and long
> drawn-out) were performed under the superinten-
> dence of Saul. He made havoc of the church for
> some time, during which occurred the first stage of
> Philip's mission in Samaria and the coast towns.
> Under the Roman law the persecution must stop
> short of the death penalty. Though occasionally
> some exceptional act of Jewish religious frenzy, such
> as Stephen's murder, might be winked at, yet the
> Roman government would not permit such acts to
> become habitual. Saul, therefore, having done all
> that was possible in Jerusalem, looked out for a new
> field of action.[2]

Saul set off for Damascus armed with the high priest's endorse-
ment. He had his sights set on followers of Christ living in that

---

2. William M. Ramsay, *St. Paul: The Traveler and Roman Citizen*, rev. ed., ed. Mark Wilson (Grand Rapids, Mich.: Kregel Publications, 2001), p. 42.

great city, which was located approximately 150 miles north of Jerusalem. Considered the oldest city in the ancient Near East, Damascus was highly esteemed as a major crossroad in the ancient world. Many Christians fled there, fearing for their safety as the flames of persecution intensified.

But on his way there, Saul's murderous mission came to an abrupt end. On a dusty road, just outside the perimeter of Damascus, the Pharisee who had been set on arresting Christians came face-to-face with the risen Christ. The book of Acts records the event as follows:

> As he was traveling, it happened that he was approaching Damascus, and suddenly a light from heaven flashed around him; and he fell to the ground and heard a voice saying to him, "Saul, Saul, why are you persecuting Me?" And he said, "Who are You, Lord?" And He said, "I am Jesus whom you are persecuting, but get up and enter the city, and it will be told you what you must do." The men who traveled with him stood speechless, hearing the voice but seeing no one. Saul got up from the ground, and though his eyes were open, he could see nothing; and leading him by the hand, they brought him into Damascus. And he was three days without sight, and neither ate nor drank. (Acts 9:3–9)

Though blinded by the light, Saul heard a voice say, "Saul, Saul, why are you persecuting Me?" He responded by calling the figure Lord. The Greek word kurios, or Lord, could be used as a title of respect and reverence for a person in authority. Quite likely, though, Saul sensed this was no mere mortal. He addressed the shining visitor as deity by asking, "Who are You, Lord?"

Saul must have been stunned to hear the reply, "I am Jesus whom you are persecuting." No longer could Saul continue under the conviction that this rebel prophet from Nazareth lay dead in an obscure tomb. He was now confronted with the risen Christ, and the trembling young Pharisee fell prostrate before the Savior. Ironically, instead of leading Christians in chains out of Damascus bound for Jerusalem, Saul was led into Damascus, his soul captive to the living Christ!

Kicking against God's Goads

Let's turn now to another passage in the book of Acts to fill in some of the details of Paul's conversion. If we look closely, we'll discover that Paul's conversion was no spur-of-the-moment encounter with God. No, the Holy Spirit had been there all along, preparing Saul for his divine appointment with Christ.

Acts 26 recounts Paul's famous defense before King Agrippa. With chains rattling and arms outstretched, the embattled apostle exclaimed:

> "While so engaged as I was journeying to Damascus with the authority and commission of the chief of priests, at midday, O King, I saw on the way a light from heaven, brighter than the sun, shining all around me and those who were journeying with me. And when we had all fallen to the ground, I heard a voice saying to me in the Hebrew dialect, 'Saul, Saul, why are you persecuting Me? It is hard for you to kick against the goads.'" (vv. 12–14)

The unusual expression "kick against the goads" rang familiar to Saul. It was a Greek proverbial phrase that referred to the goads used to prod oxen or other beasts of burden.[3] To encourage his oxen to pull harder, a farmer would use a pointed rod to prod the hind parts of the beasts. In protest, the animals would often kick against that action. The result would be a painful reminder of who was in charge.

Scholars believe that the expression testifies to the fact that Saul had not "been altogether at ease in his conscience in his persecution of Christians. We are not to think that Paul was under a great conviction of sin, for he elsewhere tells us that he persecuted

---

3. Some commentators believe the expression to be a Greek proverb that has in mind a deliberate, stubborn opposition to deity. Richard Longenecker explains: "Paul may have picked it up in Tarsus or during his missionary journeys. He used it here [Acts 26:14b] to show his Greek-oriented audience the implications of the question 'Saul, Saul, why do you persecute me?' Lest he be misunderstood as proclaiming only a Galilean prophet he had formerly opposed, he pointed out to his hearers what was obvious to any Jew: correction by a voice from heaven meant opposition to God himself. So he used a current expression familiar to Agrippa and the others." See Richard N. Longenecker, "Acts," in *The Expositor's Bible Commentary*, ed. Frank E. Gaebelein, vol. 9 (Grand Rapids, Mich.: Zondervan Publishing Company, 1981), pp. 552–53.

the church in ignorance (1 Tim. 1:13). However, deep in his mind was the nagging conviction that possibly Stephen and the other Christians were right; and the Lord now showed him that this was a divine pressure."[4]

Could there have been some divine pricks of the conscience that Saul "kicked against" all along in his resistance to the Messiah? What were the events that led up to Saul's dramatic conversion? The Bible leaves us to wonder.

First, perhaps the life and ministry of Jesus haunted the ambitious Pharisee. Because they were contemporaries, it is possible that Saul may have encountered Jesus in person before meeting Him on the Damascus road. Regardless, Saul doubtless knew of Jesus' teaching and perhaps had even heard detailed accounts of His miraculous deeds. He may have heard of and possibly even witnessed some of the events that led up to the crucifixion.

Second, Saul probably never fully recovered from taking part in Stephen's death. He may have even kept one of the robes that he held for the perpetrators as they performed their awful deed. Stained with the dried blood of the young martyr, the tattered garment may have served as a nagging reminder of Stephen's attitude as he died. Full of peace, Stephen even asked God to forgive his brutal attackers (Acts 7:60).

Third, the courage of the Christians Saul persecuted and arrested surely gave him pause. What would drive these people to align themselves with a dead man, to die for their faith in Him? Saul may have heard these followers of Jesus quote words He delivered on a crowded mountain slope in Galilee: "Blessed are those who have been persecuted for the sake of righteousness, for theirs is the kingdom of heaven. Blessed are you when people insult you and persecute you . . . because of Me. Rejoice and be glad, for your reward in heaven is great" (Matt. 5:10–12). These penetrating words may have come from the lips of the very ones he dragged off to prison and eventually had put to death. Their faith goaded his conscience.

Saul could not escape God's gracious pursuit. Ultimately, on a dusty thoroughfare north of Jerusalem, the Lord caught him, blinded him, and conquered his heart. Like the battleship captain who altered his course to avoid crashing into the lighthouse, the once-

---

4. Charles F. Pfeiffer and Everett F. Harrison, eds., *The Wycliffe Bible Commentary* (Chicago, Ill.: Moody Press, 1962), p. 1172.

self-avowed avenger of Judaism changed his course and humbly submitted to the Captain of his soul.

The rest, as we say, is history.

🖋 *Living Insights*

Most Christians can recall the events surrounding their conversion. Some remember the exact details of the moment . . . the song being sung by the choir, the weather on the day they came to know Him, even the precise words to a prayer they uttered through a veil of tears in submission to His tender calling.

And there are countless Christians alive today who experienced a dramatic conversion like Saul's on the Damascus road . . . when God in His mercy stepped into their path, changed their course, and captured their heart through Christ.

Martin Luther, the renowned leader of the Protestant Reformation, struggled for years under the guilt of his sin, desperately wanting a relationship with God but never finding it through empty religion. Then, Luther had a dramatic conversion experience. One night, alone at his bedside, he read from the book of Romans these penetrating words from the pen of Paul: "the just shall live by faith . . ." (Rom. 1:17). And in that moment, a light suddenly shone brightly in the darkness of his heart. The living Savior broke into the chamber of despair and turned on the shining light of His grace.

Two centuries later another theologian and songwriter, Charles Wesley, caught the essence of Luther's dramatic conversion in a single stanza of his hymn, "And Can It Be That I Should Gain?"

> Long my imprisoned spirit lay
> Fast bound in sin and nature's night.
> Thine eye diffused a quick'ning ray;
> I woke—the dungeon flamed with light!
> My chains fell off, my heart was free,
> I rose, went forth, and followed Thee.[5]

Regardless of the circumstances surrounding your conversion, the essence of every salvation experience is captured in Charles

---

5. Charles Wesley, "And Can It Be That I Should Gain?" in *Hymns for the Family of God* (Nashville, Tenn.: Paragon Associates Inc., 1976), pp. 260–61.

Wesley's words. When God in His grace penetrates the dark, sinful chambers of the human heart and breaks the chains of guilt, we are set free. We initiate nothing. Through Christ, God dispels our darkness and leads us into the marvelous light!

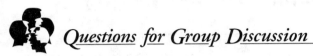 ## Questions for Group Discussion

1. Has God ever changed your course in a significant way? If so, how? How have you seen Him work in the lives of others?

2. In what ways was Saul "kicking against the goads" as he persecuted Christians? How have you felt the conviction of the Holy Spirit in your own life?

3. Why do you think Paul didn't eat or drink for three days following his radical conversion? How was his life changed as a result of meeting Christ?

4. Have you ever been persecuted for your faith? If so, how? How did these experiences affect your relationship with Christ?

Chapter 3

THE MEMORABLE FAITH OF A FORGOTTEN HERO

Acts 9:10–22

S aul of Tarsus wasn't the only one receiving unexpected visits from the Lord. There was another—a man living in Damascus named Ananias, who was a faithful follower of Jesus.

The flames of persecution had no doubt lapped closely to Ananias's door. He knew of Saul's violent background and his hatred toward all who believed in Christ. Ananias must have experienced quite a shock when the Lord appeared to him in a vision and commanded him to minister to Saul, the notorious Pharisee responsible for launching such a fiery assault on Christians.

What would you do if God commanded you to go into the fire for His cause? Would you melt away as your faith faded, or would you come through as purified gold? Keep this question in mind as you study Ananias and his memorable faith.

Saul's Surprising Commission

Though Saul was physically blind from his encounter with Jesus on the Damascus road, the eyes of his heart had been opened, and he waited to see what the Lord was going to do next. His new assignment would come through the trembling hands of Ananias, a disciple plucked from obscurity because of his great faith.

God's Call

Ananias had a vision concerning Saul, as recorded in Acts 9:

> Now there was a disciple at Damascus named Ananias; and the Lord said to him in a vision, "Ananias." And he said, "Here I am, Lord." And the Lord said to him, "Get up and go to the street called Straight, and inquire at the house of Judas for a man from Tarsus named Saul, for he is praying, and he has seen in a vision a man named Ananias come in and lay his hands on him, so that he might regain his sight." (vv. 10–12)

Thanks to Luke's narrative, we know something of this Ananias whom the Lord commanded to visit Saul. He was referred to as a disciple, a fact that reflects his unwavering commitment to Christ. The Greek word translated "disciple" here is *mathetes,* which comes from the verb *manthano,* "to learn."[1] Ananias was in the process of learning. The use of the word in this passage is particularly significant given the narrative that follows. Christ's command given to Ananias would be a genuine test of his obedience. When Jesus had commanded His followers to "go therefore and make disciples" (Matt. 28:19), His "mission was not to win loose adherents for a movement. Instead, . . . his disciples . . . were to teach those who believe 'to obey everything' he had commanded them (v. 20)."[2] This process of learning obedience was part of Ananias's journey toward spiritual maturity.

Ananias's Response

The horrifying reports of what was being done to believers in Jerusalem had undoubtedly reached as far north as Damascus. So it is not surprising that Ananias initially resisted the Lord's shocking command.

> Ananias protested, "Master, you can't be serious. Everybody's talking about this man and the terrible things he's been doing, his reign of terror against your people in Jerusalem! And now he's shown up here with papers from the Chief Priest that give him license to do the same to us." (Acts 9:13–14 THE MESSAGE)[3]

In Ananias's mind, Saul was not simply a harmless politician traversing the countryside, hoping to scare a few Christians. The Sanhedrin had charged Saul to carry out murderous deeds, granting him both authority and the resources to do so. Saul's commission had teeth! But God possessed greater power and a greater plan than Saul or the religious authorities, and no one could stand in His way.

---

1. Lawrence O. Richards, *Expository Dictionary of Bible Words* (Grand Rapids, Mich.: Zondervan Publishing House, 1985), p. 226.

2. Richards, *Expository Dictionary of Bible Words,* p. 227.

3. Eugene H. Peterson, *The Message: The Bible in Contemporary Language* (Colorado Springs., Colo.: NavPress, 2002).

But the Lord said to [Ananias], "Go, for he is a chosen instrument of Mine, to bear My name before the Gentiles and kings and the sons of Israel; for I will show him how much he must suffer for My name's sake." (vv. 15–16)

Notice the way God dealt mercifully with Ananias's reluctance and fear. He spurred him onward but also let him in on the bigger picture of His plan for Saul's ministry. These words must have convinced the reluctant Ananias to obey God's command. He obediently left to take the Lord's message to Saul.

So Ananias departed and entered the house, and after laying his hands on him said, "Brother Saul, the Lord Jesus, who appeared to you on the road by which you were coming, has sent me so that you may regain your sight and be filled with the Holy Spirit." And immediately there fell from his eyes something like scales, and he regained his sight, and he got up and was baptized; and he took food and was strengthened. (vv. 17–19)

Saul: From Raging Bull to Bleating Lamb

How fitting that the raging bull from Tarsus should be transformed into a bleating lamb through the tender ministry of a forgotten hero! Scholar Everett Harrison reflects on this poignant scene:

The first act of Ananias on entering Judas's house was to lay his hands on Saul. In the initial sense, this pertained to the healing of the blindness (compare Acts 28:8), but it had relevance also to the filling with the Spirit that is noted here (compare 8:17). The commission of verse 15 would have had little meaning apart from the divine enablement to fulfill it.

Since Ananias was not an official of the church, Saul was not put in the position of being subordinated to a "higher-up." No doubt the hands were gently applied, but what reassured Saul more than this was the opening word in his greeting: "Brother Saul." To be counted as a brother in Christ after his attempts to ruin the church must have suffused his soul with astonishment and joy. What a blessed introduction to Christian fellowship! There was no word of reproach for his persecuting activities, only a hearty welcome into the fold.[4]

What a picture of grace and forgiveness! God gently grafted the hardened Pharisee into a new family of faith. No wonder "Grace!" would be the apostle's charge as he battled to win Gentiles to Christ. The Giver of amazing grace had conquered Saul on the Damascus road, and now Ananias commissioned him as apostle to the world.

God's Plan to Use Suffering

How did God take a man notorious for his brutal past and transform him into a vessel of honor and grace? The answer lies in the words the Lord Jesus spoke when He appeared to Ananias:

> But the Lord said to him, "Go, for he is a chosen instrument of Mine, to bear My name before the Gentiles and kings and the sons of Israel; for *I will show him how much he must suffer for My name's sake.*" (Acts 9:15–16, emphasis added)

In order to comply with God's command, perhaps Ananias needed to know that suffering was part of the Lord's plan for Saul. On the anvil of suffering, often intense suffering, God forges His servants into instruments He can use. The apostle's own words later in his ministry reveal that this part of God's plan was fulfilled:

> Five times I received from the Jews thirty-nine lashes. Three times I was beaten with rods, once I was stoned, three times I was shipwrecked, a night and a day I have spent in the deep. I have been on frequent journeys, in dangers from rivers, dangers from robbers, dangers from my countrymen, dangers from the Gentiles, dangers in the city, dangers in the wilderness, dangers on the sea, dangers among false brethren; I have been in labor and hardship, through many sleepless nights, in hunger and thirst, often without food, in cold and exposure. . . .
> If I have to boast, I will boast of what pertains to my weakness. (2 Cor. 11:24–27, 30)

4. Everett F. Harrison, *Interpreting Acts: The Expanding Church* (Grand Rapids, Mich.: Academic Books, Zondervan Publishing House, 1986), pp. 163–64.

The apostle progressed from intense suffering to boasting in weakness. Saul made this connection regularly in his epistles to the churches.

Hardship gave Saul's mission credibility. It would take supernatural intervention—a divine regimen of intense suffering—to develop the determined Pharisee into a gracious, humble servant of the Lord. Only God could do that. But Saul's call and his baptism (Acts 9:18) were just the beginning of what God had in store for the newly appointed apostle.

A Remarkable Transformation

By God's grace, the once-vengeful Pharisee became an ambassador for Christ. And it wasn't long before he began to boldly proclaim the very Gospel he had once violently opposed.

> Now for several days he was with the disciples who were at Damascus, and immediately he began to proclaim Jesus in the synagogues, saying, "He is the Son of God." All those hearing him continued to be amazed, and were saying, "Is this not he who in Jerusalem destroyed those who called on this name, and who had come here for the purpose of bringing them bound before the chief priests?" But Saul kept increasing in strength and confounding the Jews who lived at Damascus by proving that this Jesus is the Christ. (Acts 9:19–22)

How's that for a genuine illustration of the power of God? The people listening to Saul's preaching reacted with astonishment. The word Luke used, translated here "amazed," comes from the Greek word *existemi*, which in this form means a "feeling of astonishment mingled with fear, caused by events which are miraculous, extraordinary, or difficult to understand."[5]

As the spiritually minded synagogue attendees listened to Saul preach, they sensed the power of the Divine. It amazed, even frightened them. It was obvious that something supernatural and miraculous had occurred in Saul's life. Saul led his Jewish audiences

---

5. William F. Arndt and F. Wilbur Gingrich, eds., *A Greek-English Lexicon of the New Testament and Other Early Christian Literature,* 2d ed. (Chicago, Ill.: The University of Chicago Press, 1979), p. 276.

logically through the familiar Hebrew Scriptures, yet he opened up the truths of the Word of God for them in a fresh, new way. He delivered an irrefutable case for trusting in Jesus as the promised Messiah. Through Saul's moving message, the Spirit pierced hearts and convicted many souls.

Four Lessons on Faith

But let's not forget . . . perhaps none of this would have transpired without Ananias's obedience to God's astonishing plan. Just let that fact sink in for a few moments. Ananias's faith impacted the destiny of millions! Ours can too. We just need to understand some of the surprising elements of God's will.

First, *surprises are always part of God's leading.* Both Saul and Ananias experienced surprising visits from the Lord. It's unlikely that the Lord will meet *us* on the road or visit us at the foot of our bed in a vision to announce His plans. However, He may lead in a way that is unexpected. A new job. A new baby. A move. An unexpected promotion. A layoff. A quiet, gentle nudging in a ministry direction we never thought possible. Whatever the case, God's plan often comes as a surprise to His children. He may require us to trust Him the way Abraham did, when he "obeyed by going out to a place which he was to receive for an inheritance; and he went out, *not knowing where he was going*" (Heb. 11:8, emphasis added).

Second, *surprises always intensify our need for faith.* The serendipitous element of God's leading forces us to engage at a new level of faith. As in Ananias's story, at times fear accompanies the realization of the Lord's leading. But faith allows us to overcome that initial fearful response and step into the future with confidence. When we respond in obedience to God's will, we live by faith and not by sight!

Third, *stepping out in faith always results in further clarification of God's plan.* The first step always presents the greatest challenge! But once we take that faith step, God will reveal what our next step should be. And the next. And the next. He gives us the information and guidance we need so that we can move forward in faith, pursuing Him and His will with all our hearts. Ananias discovered this when God revealed inside information to him regarding Saul. God informed his humble servant that Saul was His "chosen instrument," whom He had chosen to bear His name before Gentiles, kings, and Jews alike. You won't receive such insights if you're hanging back in the security and safety of the status quo, but when you step out, more is revealed. Once you receive God's clear guidance, then take the faith leap!

Finally, *obedience always stimulates growth.* In contrast, disobedience stunts spiritual growth. Through obedience we gain maturity, and our faith flourishes! Psalm 1 likens a faithful believer to a lovely tree firmly planted near streams of water. When we obey God consistently, our spiritual roots sink deep into the rich soil of God's Word. No wind or raging torrent can uproot our faith from its solid foundation.

When we embrace these four principles, just as Ananias did, we'll begin to see positive spiritual results. Obedience encourages us to go deeper with God. As we learn to expect blessings and surprises from the hand of our heavenly Father, we will faithfully anticipate the work He plans to do in our lives instead of dreading the unknown. He will lovingly pry our fingers away from worldly pleasures, consuming relationships, and lesser commitments as He molds us into stronger, more mature, more disciplined believers. As a result, we'll no longer be labeled *fearful.* Instead, we'll be called *faithful.*

Living Insights

Take some time to go back and read through Acts 9:1–22. Imagine being a Jewish Christian living in Damascus under the threat of being imprisoned for your faith. Look closely at verses 1–9 and compare them to verses 10–16. Compare and contrast Saul's encounter with Jesus with Ananias's vision from God. What words or images are the same? Different?

_____

_____

_____

What have you learned from the story of Ananias about being a genuine disciple of Jesus? How does his story challenge you in your own relationship with the Lord?

_____

_____

Describe a time when the Lord led you in an unexpected direction. How did you respond? In what ways does your story of responding to God's surprising leading compare to Ananias's? In what ways does it differ?

Perhaps the Lord has challenged you today to a level of obedience you've never experienced before. Maybe He's leading you to make a difficult decision . . . to break a stubborn pattern . . . to end or start a relationship . . . to begin a new ministry. This is your opportunity to experience His power and provision by obeying in faith. You really can trust Him! Go ahead and take that first step. Commit your plan to the Lord, and trust Him to take care of the details!

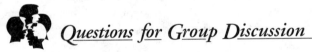 ## Questions *for* Group Discussion

1. Have you ever been skeptical of a person's conversion like Ananias was of Saul's? If so, why were you doubtful? What eventually happened in that person's life?

2. How did God use the situation with Saul to test Ananias's faith? How do you think this changed Ananias's walk with God?

3. What was the significance of Saul's blindness? What do you think God was teaching him through the experience? How did it change him?

4. Name a time when God called you to step out in faith and obey Him, even when you were fearful. What were the circumstances? What did you learn as a result of this experience?

Chapter 4

THE NECESSITY OF SOLITUDE, QUIETNESS, AND OBSCURITY

Galatians 1:10–17

> Superficiality is the curse of our age. The doctrine of instant satisfaction is a primary spiritual problem. The desperate need today is not for a greater number of intelligent people, or gifted people, but for deep people.[1] —Richard Foster

Let's face it—our society places little value on the deeper life. Frantic schedules, long hours at work, marital conflicts, back-breaking debt, poor diet, little exercise, the pursuit of material success, and a lack of accountability deplete our reservoirs of energy, character, and integrity to dangerously low levels. The result? Superficial, shallow lives.

Depth of character is developed in solitude, quietness, and obscurity. But in our frenzied world of busyness and ambition, little time remains for cultivating our inner lives. God must be grieved over this because He designed us to run deep! The Bible is full of examples of individuals who learned through protracted periods of solitude, quietness, and obscurity the value of going deep. They needed time alone with God in the wilderness.

Biblical Retreatants at a Glance

You may already be thinking of some of God's servants who cultivated the deeper life through the disciplines of solitude and quietness before the Lord. Let's look more closely at a few.

Moses. At the pinnacle of his career as an Egyptian royal, Moses committed a murder that sent him running for his life into obscurity. For forty years he wandered the plains of Midian tending sheep. Not until he was eighty years old did God deem him ready for the task of rescuing the Israelites from slavery. His preparation took place in the wilderness.

---

1. Richard J. Foster, *Celebration of Discipline: The Path to Spiritual Growth*, 3d ed. (San Francisco, Calif.: HarperSanFrancisco, HarperCollins Publishers, 1998), p. 1.

David. Though anointed king of Israel as a teen, David spent decades waiting to take his throne. He knew what it was like to be a lonely, frustrated fugitive in the wilderness. Yet in those dark times he penned many of the psalms, some of the best-loved verses of the entire Bible. During his periods of waiting, David learned to meet God, to pray, to sing praises, to rise above his circumstances, and to trust God in the dark. God even called him "a man after My own heart." This shepherd-king gained spiritual depth through his desert experiences.

Joseph. Joseph was hurled headlong from riches to rags because of the foolish rant of a scorned woman. Because of her accusations, he waited in jail for years, wondering if God had forgotten him. But God didn't forget! He restored Joseph to a position of greatness and influence because of his obedience and his refusal to compromise God's principles.

Elijah. After delivering God's message of judgment to King Ahab, Elijah hid in the desert. The parched ground on which he lay reflected the spiritual drought in Elijah's heart. In this remote setting, God renewed the weary prophet's spirit and prepared him for the challenges ahead.

John the Baptist. This young, gifted preacher spent years proclaiming God's Word. He was destined for greatness by sheer virtue of his pedigree, but God had another plan. God's preparation for the prophet's powerful ministry included that time in the desert, away from the crowds. There, he learned that his ministry was not about himself; it was about preparing the way for another. John the Baptist gained a rare humility as he wandered in the desert, waiting for God's plan to unfold.

Saul's Desert Retreat

Saul-turned-Paul, the great proclaimer of grace, had a similar story. The converted Pharisee learned crucial lessons of submission and humility in the silence and obscurity of his own desert retreat.

In Galatians 1, Paul recounted his experience. He was quick to point out his own attitude shift—a result of his time in the wilderness:

> For am I now seeking the favor of men, or of God? Or am I striving to please men? If I were still trying to please men, I would not be a bond-servant of Christ. (Gal. 1:10)

Notice the phrase "still trying to please men" in verse 10. Plagued with a relentless drive to please people, Saul longed for the approving nod of the Sanhedrin. He loved applause, seeking after approving words and accolades from men. But all this changed on the road to Damascus. Saul's perspective altered as he stopped focusing on what he had been doing and realized what God had done. Take a look at the words he used next:

> But when God, who had set me apart even from my mother's womb and called me through His grace, was pleased to reveal His Son in me so that I might preach Him among the Gentiles, I did not immediately consult with flesh and blood, nor did I go up to Jerusalem to those who were apostles before me; but *I went away to Arabia,* and returned once more to Damascus. (vv. 15–17, emphasis added)

In this passage, Paul addressed two things he did not do. First, he "did not immediately consult with flesh and blood" (v. 16). He resisted the strong temptation to seek the company or advice of others who might not have understood his situation. This way, he had time to process the events that had occurred without being influenced by other people.

Second, Paul pointed out that he did not rush to Jerusalem to present himself to the apostles in hopes of gaining quick access to their ranks. Commentator Leon Morris explains why Paul emphasized this point:

> This emphatic disclaimer of any contact with earlier believers and their leaders makes it clear that Paul did not derive his understanding of the Christian message from any who were Christians before him. Specifically, he did not learn from, nor was he commissioned by, those who had been apostles before him. It could not be said that he had had instruction and had misunderstood what earlier teachers were trying to convey to him. It is of primary importance for Paul that he had been directly commissioned by Jesus.[2]

You may be wondering where Saul received all this remarkable

---

2. Leon Morris, *Galatians: Paul's Charter of Christian Freedom* (Downers Grove, Ill.: Inter-Varsity Press, 1996), p. 57.

theological and spiritual insight. He gleaned it through time spent with the Lord—through prayer, fasting, and spiritual discipline. Saul gained obedience and maturity from his sabbatical in the desert of Arabia.

The Place of Arabia

Arabia stretched from as far south as Sinai near Egypt north to the southern edges of Syria. Its borders may have nestled against the city limits of Damascus. Some scholars believe the close proximity of the city to the desert expanse makes this the likely location of Saul's retreat. This area was a barren wilderness. Saul's years spent there contrasted sharply with the glamorous existence of an up-and-coming Pharisee.

Why go to the desert? Couldn't Saul have learned the same essential qualities of character in the seclusion of his home in Tarsus? Perhaps. But in this case, that wasn't God's plan.

The Purpose of Arabia

For three years—over one thousand days—Saul lived in solitude in this bleak wilderness (see Gal. 1:18). No crowds. No applause. No glowing accolades from the ranks of the Sanhedrin. Only time alone to pray, to meditate, to commune with his Savior. Perhaps this is where he began to conclude what he would later write:

> Whatever things were gain to me, those things I have counted as loss for the sake of Christ. More than that, I count all things to be loss in view of the surpassing value of knowing Christ Jesus my Lord, for whom I have suffered the loss of all things, and count them but rubbish so that I may gain Christ. (Phil. 3:7–8)

Such depth of resolve could only be the result of a protracted period of cultivating the hidden life. For Saul, the desert became a holy place.

> Arabia became a temple where he worshiped the Lord in a way he had never experienced in his life. Solitude helped. . . . As the desert winds howled across rocky gorges, God revealed Himself to His servant.[3]

3. Charles R. Swindoll, *Paul: A Man of Grace and Grit* (Nashville, Tenn.: The W Publishing Group, 2002), pp. 55–56.

Prescription for Growing Deep

Having reflected on Saul's desert experience, let's explore three strategies that can help us make some radical yet essential adjustments.

First, *instead of speeding up, slow down and rethink.* Slowing down takes more than a commitment; it takes discipline. For you, that may mean sitting down with your mate, your family, or on your own to do some honest reflecting on the pace of your life. What is the condition of your spiritual life? Which outside activities are essential? Which are not? How can you adjust your routine to make slowing down a priority? Answering these tough questions honestly will pay rich dividends as you invest in your inner life.

Second, *instead of talking more, be quiet and reflect.* God's still, small voice is too often drowned out by the din and clamor of living. We can't hear Him because we're either tuned in to other voices or we're too busy listening to ourselves. Neither promises eternal benefits. Being quiet and reflecting regularly allows God an opportunity to speak to our hearts . . . and a time for us to listen.

Third, *instead of seeking a place of power, be still and release.* This applies to everyone and especially to those involved in vocational Christian service. One pastor made this penetrating observation:

> I've hung around the training of ministers long enough to know that there can be an enormous amount of envy among individuals in our line of work. Insecurity surfaces as competition abounds. The push for power is so evident it's sickening. No doubt the same sort of silly battles with pride and prestige exist in other professions as well.[4]

For Saul, the battle against worldly ambition was fought and won on the Damascus road. The discipline of remaining in submission to his new Master, however, came while he waited in the desert. When we come face-to-face with Christ and then walk with Him in quietness and solitude, we'll gain the same attitude of submission.

Saul learned this lesson and many more during his years of solitude in Arabia. Only after a season of deep, honest reflection and intimate communion with the Lord was he ready to begin his mission for Christ. Are you ready to begin yours?

4. Swindoll, *Paul*, p. 58.

✒ Living Insights

Author Ken Gire writes,

> Much of what is sacred is hidden in the ordinary, everyday moments of our lives. To see something of the sacred in those moments takes slowing down so we can live our lives more reflectively.
>
> The word *reflect* comes from two Latin words: *re*, meaning "back," and *flectere*, meaning "to bend." To reflect, then, is to bend back something, like the way a mirror bends back an image, providing an opportunity for a closer look. Living reflectively provides opportunities during our day for a closer look at things, at people, at ourselves, and at God.[5]

Name an occasion when God used a time of solitude, quietness, and reflection to speak to your heart. What was the situation, and what happened as a result?

_____

_____

_____

_____

_____

How much time do you currently spend praying, thinking, and reflecting each day? How do you set the scene for your encounters with God?

_____

_____

_____

_____

_____

5. Ken Gire, *The Reflective Life: Becoming More Spiritually Sensitive to the Everyday Moments of Life* (Colorado Springs, Colo.: Chariot Victor Publishing, 1998), p. 25.

If you don't have much time in your current schedule for reflection, how can you rearrange your priorities to make more time?

_____

_____

_____

_____

_____

_____

How can you integrate the principles mentioned in this chapter into your relationships with God, your spouse, your family, and other loved ones?

_____

_____

_____

_____

_____

_____

 ## Questions _for_ Group Discussion

1. How did God use Saul's time in the desert to prepare him for ministry? What lessons have you learned from his example?

2. How do you practice the spiritual disciplines of reflection and solitude in your own life? In what areas do you need encouragement? How can you encourage others in your group?

3. Has God used solitude and silence to speak to you in the past? What impact did this have on your spiritual life?

4. What do you do to retreat into solitude and quietness with the Lord? Pair up with a partner to pray, and set a time for yourself to spend in reflection and prayer each day. Ask your partner to help you remain accountable in keeping this a priority.

Chapter 5

MISSION UNDERWAY...
THANKS TO THE
LESSER-KNOWN

Acts 9:3–31

William Ernest Henley captured the height of humanism when he wrote these words at the end of the nineteenth century:

> Out of the night that covers me,
> Black as the Pit from pole to pole,
> I thank whatever gods may be
> For my unconquerable soul.
>
> In the fell clutch of circumstance
> I have not winced nor cried aloud.
> Under the bludgeonings of chance
> My head is bloody, but unbowed. . . .
>
> It matters not how strait the gate,
> How charged with punishments the scroll,
> I am the master of my fate:
> *I am the captain of my soul.*[1]

Nice poem. Abominable theology! Good for graduation speeches, horrible for Christian living. While the world says, "Fly solo," God says, "Take a backseat." Whether in the executive office, in the marketplace, or on your cul-de-sac, society exalts independence. God prizes dependence. You may have heard the saying "God helps those who help themselves." Nice thought, but you'll never find it in Scripture. God helps the helpless, the destitute, and those who are dependent on Him.

From the time we're born our quest for autonomy begins. We learn to walk, and suddenly it's time to explore the vast ocean of a shopping mall without Mommy's hand. We learn to talk, and it's not long before we're saying, "Let me do it by myself!" As a teenager,

---

1. William Ernest Henley, "Invictus," as quoted by Charles R. Swindoll in *Paul: A Man of Grace and Grit* (Nashville, Tenn.: The W Publishing Group, 2002), pp. 62–63.

our freedom is defined by two words—*driver's license*. As we grow up, we strive to make a name for ourselves, max out our potential, and conquer our struggles alone. But once we turn toward Christ, independence is no longer an option. He asks us to be as dependent on Him as a baby in the womb. It's a tough lesson for all believers to learn, but it's a lesson of love. God sent Saul of Tarsus on just such a crash course.

For young Saul, God drove out any hope of independence in three distinct stages: in blindness, in obscurity, and in danger.

Blindness: Stopped in His Tracks

In his zeal, Saul desired to expand the extermination of Christians to Damascus—one of the most significant cities in the ancient Near East and a trading center on the edge of the desert. But, as chapter 2 described, God stopped him in his tracks:

> As he was traveling, it happened that he was approaching Damascus, and suddenly a light from heaven flashed around him. . . . Saul got up from the ground, and though his eyes were open, he could see nothing; and leading him by the hand, [his companions] brought him to Damascus. (Acts 9:3, 8)

One minute this self-built man was walking on a self-appointed mission; the next he was groveling in submission. Blindness forced Saul to depend on someone else to lead him like a child into the city. This proud Pharisee wasn't used to being led anywhere by the hand—he was the one to lead others! Saul's companions dropped him off in an unknown room, leaving him there blind and alone.

> And he was three days without sight, and neither ate nor drank. (v. 9)

Not only was Saul completely alone, but he had also lost his appetite. His supernatural encounter with God had shaken him indeed.

Before his experience on the Damascus road, Saul needed no one. *He* set the agenda. *He* ran the show. *He* was master of his fate and captain of his soul. Now he couldn't even find his way around the room without assistance. While Saul waited for further instructions and fasted in darkness, God appointed a stranger to minister to him.

A Guide to the Blind

As we saw in chapter 3, God commissioned Ananias to instruct Saul regarding his new allegiance, new purpose, and new plan for his life. God never intended Saul to go solo. In the darkness, Saul felt on his shoulders the hands of this complete stranger and heard a voice calling him "Brother Saul" for the first time:

> So Ananias departed and entered the house, and after laying his hands on him said, "Brother Saul, the Lord Jesus, who appeared to you on the road by which you were coming, has sent me so that you may regain your sight and be filled with the Holy Spirit." (v. 17)

"Brother . . ." Like the first cool breeze breaking the heat of summer, that one word brought an end to Saul's three days of loneliness, confusion, and fear. What a humbling affirmation for this former murderer! Immediately after Saul was baptized into the family of God, he and Ananias shared a meal. Fitting, isn't it? Family sharing life together. We need people each step of our Christian journey. For Saul, it was just the beginning of his transformation from former captain of his own soul to deckhand on God's ship.

From Persecutor to Preacher

Thanks to the assistance of another, Saul gained five key benefits: (1) he regained his sight, (2) he received an explanation of what had happened, (3) he was filled with the Holy Spirit, (4) he took food and was strengthened, and (5) he was introduced to other believers in Damascus.

> Now for several days he was with the disciples who were at Damascus. (v. 19b)

Saul's passion to persecute Christians had quickly transformed into a passion to proclaim Christ:

> And *immediately* he began to proclaim Jesus in the synagogues, saying, "He is the Son of God." (v. 20, emphasis added)

What a testimony! Imagine this up-and-coming Pharisee now preaching the Gospel to his former Jewish companions. Confounding the religious leaders and growing in faith, Saul would have been a marketing dream to the early Christians. In our day, slick ad campaigns with catchy slogans like, "Christian-killer turned Christ-follower!" would be plastered on billboards, aired on Christian radio stations, and printed in Christian magazines. But instead of popularity, God gave Saul obscurity. The young convert needed to learn outside the spotlight, in a seminary surrounded by sand.

Obscurity: A Trip to the Desert

As we learned in the previous chapter, God used Saul's desert sojourn to grow him, to cultivate in him the deeper life, and to allow him to learn from the Lord Himself.

As a Pharisee, Saul would have memorized virtually all thirty-nine books of our Old Testament. Now, as a new believer, Saul could put the face of Christ onto the pages of Isaiah, Psalms, and Malachi. His knowledge of Scripture was now infused with the life of Christ.

When we think of the apostle Paul, or any strong mouthpiece for God, we usually think of his countless accomplishments, not his times of anonymity. We think of his later years rather than his early years. We remember Paul writing thirteen New Testament books, his preaching at the Areopagus, and his passion for mentoring young leaders. We tend to gloss over the months and months Saul spent alone in the desert of Arabia—obscure, forgotten, with howling winds swirling about him. That's how God crafts character— in solitary dependence on Him.

Danger: Escape from Former Friends, Skeptics, and New Enemies

Remember the prophecy from God to Ananias, "I will show [Saul] how much he must suffer for My name's sake" (v. 16)? On the surface, Saul's life after conversion was anything but attractive. God struck Saul with blindness and led him into obscurity for three years. Then, when Saul returned to Damascus after Arabia, he learned that he needed to depend upon God for his very life.

Escape from Former Friends

When many days had elapsed, the Jews plotted together to do away with him, but their plot became known to Saul. They were also watching the gates day and night so that they might put him to death; but his disciples took him by night and let him down through an opening in the wall, lowering him in a large basket. (vv. 23–25)

Saul's former Jewish colleagues never forgot him. As soon as he entered the gates of Damascus, they were ready to give him a traitor's welcome. Notice that even though Saul knew of the plot, it was his new disciples who improvised a plan.

John Pollock, in his book *The Man Who Shook the World*, described this scene:

His disciples took him at night to a friendly family who lived on the city walls in one of the private houses with windows jutting some eight or ten feet above the ground. They found a fish basket, a large shapeless sack which folded round his body so no casual observer would notice in the darkness that it hid a man. In the small hours they lowered him to the ground. . . .

. . . The crusade on which he had embarked so gloriously had come to a summary stop; the appointed leader was a fugitive already. . . .

. . . The irony was not lost on him that the mighty Paul who had originally approached Damascus with all the panoply of the High Priest's representative should make his last exit in a fish basket, helped by the very people he had come to hurt.[2]

God's plan baffled all reason! So Saul retreated in search of a safe harbor within the strong church in Jerusalem.

Escape from Skeptics

When [Paul] came to Jerusalem, he was trying to associate with the disciples; but they were all afraid of him, not believing that he was a disciple. (Acts 9:26)

---

2. John Pollock, *The Man Who Shook the World* (Wheaton, Ill.: Victor Books, SP Publications Inc., 1974), p. 29.

Even three to four years after his conversion, the disciples in Jerusalem reacted to Saul much like Ananias did—with skepticism. If not for a man whose very name meant "encouragement," Saul's journey might have ended before it started:

> But Barnabas took hold of him and brought him to the apostles and described to them how he had seen the Lord on the road, and that He had talked to him, and how at Damascus he had spoken out boldly in the name of Jesus. (v. 27)

Once again, Saul depended on the courage of a stranger who came alongside him. Notice the imagery in the words "took hold of him." Barnabas pulled Saul close and stood as an advocate and eventual mentor for him.

Escape from New Enemies

After Barnabas came to the rescue, it didn't take long for Saul to find another pulpit:

> And he was with them, moving about freely in Jerusalem, speaking out boldly in the name of the Lord. And he was talking and arguing with the Hellenistic Jews; but they were attempting to put him to death. But when the brethren learned of it, they brought him down to Caesarea and sent him away to Tarsus. (vv. 28–30)

As soon as Saul got a following in Damascus, he was shipped to the desert; as soon as he returned to Damascus, he slipped out like a fugitive. In Jerusalem, Barnabas took him under his wing, and then Saul began with a ministry to the Hellenistic Jews. Then, the brethren sent him off to the place of his birth—Tarsus. Saul, once the center of attention, was relegated to the sidelines, away from the action. Who would have thought that about five years after Saul's miraculous conversion, he would end up in Tarsus, separated from all the action of church growth? Notice what the passage says next:

> So the church throughout all Judea and Galilee and Samaria enjoyed peace, being built up . . . it continued to increase. (v. 31)

But Saul wasn't even there! Who, then, is responsible for church growth? Not a powerful preacher, but an omnipotent God.

Three Lessons

God stripped Saul of independence early on in his life. In blindness, obscurity, and danger, Saul learned some valuable lessons that would mark the rest of his ministry. They serve us even today:

Value others. Rather than seeing others as those who hold us back, we need to discover that they are the secret to our survival and our success. On his missionary journeys, Paul never traveled alone. God did not intend for us to tackle this life alone. Chances are He has provided acquaintances, friends, colleagues, or family members to come alongside you. Learn to value those He sends your way. Let them encourage you.

Humble yourself. Solomon wrote, "Let another praise you, and not your own mouth; a stranger, and not your own lips" (Prov. 27:2). God calls us to humility before Him and the world. The apostle Peter wrote, "Humble yourselves under the mighty hand of God, that He may exalt you at the proper time" (1 Pet. 5:6). Let God exalt you in His time. God sees you. He knows the way you take, and He uses broken vessels of humility (2 Cor. 4:6–7).

Trust God. Rather than considering ourselves indispensable (even secretly), we need to continually remind ourselves that the Lord's work must be done the Lord's way. With his talents, Saul could have forced his way into the limelight, flaunted his gifts, or pushed his agenda on others. Instead, he waited. He listened. He let the Lord work in His way. Instead of taking matters into our own hands when we feel desperate and anxious, let's take time to pull back and trust Him.

William Ernest Henley had it wrong. We are not the captains of our souls or the masters of our fate. Only One controls the intricacies of our destinies. He's the same One who delivered baby Moses in a basket from the hand of Pharaoh and delivered Saul in a basket from the hand of angry Jews. He will deliver us.

When we live in a state of independence, God takes us to Damascus. He blinds us with His light, He sends us into obscurity, or He allows us to go through a crisis. He wants us to come face-to-face with the reality that our very breath is dependent on Him. God will not be shoved off the throne by the almighty "I."

✒ _Living Insights_

John Donne wrote, "No man is an island."[3] Yet even in our church pews, we congregate like islands in an archipelago, connected by proximity but separated by waters of independence.

We sit alone, unwilling to depend on our fellow brothers and sisters in Christ. We strive to "have it together," prove our spirituality, and appear on the surface strong, solid, and independent. We strap on self-determination like a sword. We don the armor of invulnerability. And, when crisis hits our island, our very isolation prohibits any rescuers from reaching us.

Who knows you well enough to see the signs of unhealthy isolation in your life?

_____

_____

How highly do you value other people in your life? When has someone encouraged you like Barnabas encouraged Saul? When have you come alongside someone else with a word of encouragement?

_____

_____

_____

_____

_____

Think about the last time you honored a mentor or a trusted friend. Take time to thank them for their influence by writing them a note, inviting them to dinner, or sharing your gratitude in another creative way.

3. John Donne, "Meditation XVII," at http://garnet.indstate.edu/ilnprof/ENG451/ISLAND/text.html, accessed on October 25, 2002.

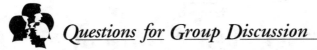 *Questions for Group Discussion*

1. Define *success*. In what areas of your life do you feel the most successful? The least successful? Why?

2. How did Saul's attitude change regarding his former success and accomplishments? What caused this radical change in his life?

3. How did Saul's background and accomplishments uniquely prepare him for the ministry to which God called him?

4. Name a time when your faith was tested and you had to depend solely on God. What happened? How did this situation impact your spiritual walk?

5. Is there a situation in your life now in which you find it difficult to truly depend on God? If so, what is it? Take time now to share with others and to offer this issue to the Lord in prayer.

Chapter 6

OUT OF THE SHADOWS

Acts 11:19–26

Admit it, you try to guess. Before Paul Harvey ever utters those immortal words, "Now you know the *rest of the story*," you rack your brain to try and guess the famous celebrity before he finally divulges the name.

The formula is relatively simple—start with the beginning of someone's life rather than the end. It works because we usually only notice people once they become famous. But without the beginning, there would be no end. More often than not, many who achieve a great deal of influence have stumbled through shadows of anonymity for long periods of time.

A British author named James Stalker summarized these situations: "Waiting is a common instrument of providential discipline for those to whom exceptional work has been appointed."[1] We all desire to accomplish the exceptional, but we want it without wrestling in the shadows, without the work, and without the waiting. We strive to be a combination of Winston Churchill, Billy Graham, Elisabeth Eliot, Bill Gates, and Mother Teresa. And we expect it all *now!*

But God doesn't work that way. Scripture teaches us an invaluable principle: *Exceptional work is preceded by extended waiting.* In fact, you will try your patience to find phrases such as "hurry up" or "it's now or never" in the Bible. Instead, you'll discover two predominant words: *wait* and *rest.*

> *Rest* in the Lord and *wait* patiently for Him.
> (Psalm 37:7, emphasis added)

> My soul, *wait* in silence for God only, for my hope is from Him. (Psalm 62:5, emphasis added)

> *Wait* for your God continually. (Hosea 12:6, emphasis added)

---

1. James Stalker, as quoted by Charles R. Swindoll in *Paul: A Man of Grace and Grit* (Nashville, Tenn.: The W Publishing Group, 2002), p. 78.

Saul in the Shadows

Perhaps these verses reverberated through Saul's mind as he pitched tents in his hometown of Tarsus. Up to this point in our study of Saul, rather than soaring to exceptional work, he has stumbled through extended periods of waiting. He's nearing middle age (probably early forties). Following a miraculous conversion and commissioning by Jesus Himself, Saul's first outings as a preacher met more resistance than revival. After three years in the desert of Arabia and a lukewarm welcome from the apostles in Jerusalem, Saul might have wondered if his experience on the Damascus road was simply a hallucination from a bad migraine. Where was the glory, the miraculous moving of God's hand, that should accompany Christian service?

> The best years of Paul's life were slipping away between the Taurus Mountains and the sea. It was harder to bear because he cared so deeply that all men everywhere should hear and believe, yet during his later thirties and into the early forties when a man approaches his prime, Paul drops out of history.[2]

Do you ever feel like you're gifted and called, but you are just circling the runway because God hasn't cleared you to land anywhere? Do you ever feel like you're on the sidelines of ministry while everyone else is in the game? Perhaps you're wondering— and maybe you're getting worried—that this waiting period might be permanent. You've just stepped into Tarsus with Saul. God hasn't forgotten about you. Remember: *Exceptional work is preceded by extended waiting.* While God shines His sovereign spotlight on some, at the same time He's forging character in others through the fires of obscurity. As often is the case, we wait; He works.

Spotlight on Peter

As we look at Acts 11, we'll notice that God's spotlight shifts from Saul to Peter. Through a dream, Peter's eyes were opened to the Gentile way of life. In a vision of a veritable feast of nonkosher foods, God told Peter to eat freely. What was once considered

---

2. John Pollock, *The Apostle: A Life of Paul* (Colorado Springs, Colo.: Cook Communications Ministries, 1985), p. 51.

unholy in the Old Testament now was cleansed by the blood of Christ (Acts 10:15).

Though God commissioned Saul as the "apostle to the Gentiles" in Acts 9:15, it was Peter in Acts 10:34–48 who reaped the first significant Gentile harvest. When Peter recounted his experience to the believers in Jerusalem (Acts 11:1–17), they glorified God and determined to share the Good News not only with Jews but with Gentiles as well.

> This is a crucial hinge in the Acts account. For the first time the church actively proselytized Gentiles. The Samaritans of chapter 8 were partly Jewish; the Ethiopian eunuch on his own was reading Isaiah 53 on his return from Jerusalem; and even Cornelius took the initiative in seeking the gospel from Peter's lips. But here the church took the first steps to take the message to uncircumcised Greeks.[3]

The wildfires of grace spread rapidly along the Mediterranean coast. Starting from the shores of Phoenicia, the Gospel was taken across the sea to the island of Cyprus and then back to the port town of Antioch (Acts 11:19–20).

Spotlight on Barnabas

Up to this point, the revival was led by "those who were scattered because of the persecution that occurred in connection with Stephen" (v. 19). In reaction to such astounding growth, the church in Jerusalem responded.

> But there were some of them, men of Cyprus and Cyrene, who came to Antioch and began speaking to the Greeks also, preaching the Lord Jesus. And the hand of the Lord was with them, and a large number who believed turned to the Lord. The news about them reached the ears of the church at Jerusalem, and *they sent Barnabas off to Antioch.* (vv. 20–22, emphasis added)

---

3. John F. Walvoord, *The Bible Knowledge Commentary: An Exposition of the Scriptures,* Acts 11:19 (Wheaton, Ill.: Victor Books, 1983/1985), vol. 2, accessed through the Logos Library System.

Why Barnabas? He was the natural choice. In Acts 4:36 we learn of his Cyprian heritage. Antioch, a major port town near Cyprus, was filled with people going to and from the island. Barnabas knew the culture, he knew the language, and he could earn trust quickly among the people. He turned out to be the right man in the right place at the right time:

> Then when [Barnabas] arrived and witnessed the grace of God, he rejoiced and began to encourage them all with resolute heart to remain true to the Lord; for he was a good man, and full of the Holy Spirit and of faith. And considerable numbers were brought to the Lord. (vv. 23–24)

Notice Barnabas "witnessed" the revival. He didn't cause it. This man supported and encouraged those impacted by God's irresistible grace. God's presence was electric! Genuine work was being done in the hearts of both Jews and Gentiles. This was a magnificent experience, and it was the work of God alone.

It's natural for us to want to reconstruct this explosion of faith in our own church setting, but you won't find the "ten principles of church growth" used at Antioch. We can't duplicate it because we didn't create it. We can willingly submit to God and allow Him to use us as we respond in obedience. Like Barnabas, we can encourage others, but it's the Lord, through His Spirit, who ignites revival.

Preparation for the Spotlight

Something miraculous was happening in Antioch! During all of this church growth, it seemed natural to ask the question, "What happened to Saul?" He's conspicuously absent here. With his clear calling, his gifts, and his passion, we would expect Saul to be at the nerve center of this revival. But he was miles away in Tarsus. Though it was his hometown, it didn't feel like home. His strong Jewish family more than likely disowned him after his conversion. The Jewish authorities probably hounded him like a wanted criminal. Later in his life, Paul reflected on this sojourn in the shadows when he wrote to the Galatians:

> Then I went into the regions of Syria and Cilicia [where Tarsus is located]. And I was *still unknown* by sight to the churches of Judea which were in Christ. (Gal. 1:21–22, emphasis added)

Saul was in the shadows, unrecognized by other Christians. Ever feel like that? Anonymous? Unknown? Perhaps you are gifted, educated, and passionate for Christ, but no one seems to notice. It's easy to crave the spotlight when we are spending time in the shadows. But unless we embrace the shadows, God will not be able to fully prepare us for the spotlight. It's not easy to embrace times of anonymity. The shadows can be a place of great pain, great discipline, great waiting . . . but also great preparation. God uses these times for His glory. This is what was happening to Saul. What was he doing during this time? We can assume that

- he was back with his family, either getting reunited or being disowned by them—probably the latter.

- he was reading much and becoming increasingly familiar with the Gentile world from which he had been separated for most of his life.

- he was encountering tension from the synagogue because of his radical new views.

- he was probably being severely disciplined by the Jews for entering Gentile homes and other establishments—that meant flogging!

- he was receiving revelation from the Lord and insight regarding his "thorn in the flesh," which was already beginning to cause him pain (see 2 Cor. 12 and chapter 7 of this guide).

It's when we are hidden in the shadows that God does His best work in us. Through the painful pricks of a thorn, God molded Saul into Paul. Once self-sufficient, he was now God-dependent. Once strong, he was now weak. In waiting we realize where true strength resides.

Barnabas Snatches Saul from the Shadows

Back in Antioch, Barnabas could barely keep his head above water. Swamped with converts, he needed help.

> And he left for Tarsus to look for Saul; and when he had found him, he brought him to Antioch. (Acts 11:25–26a)

Notice Saul never sent Barnabas a résumé. He never petitioned Barnabas with, "You know, it's pretty rough out here in Tarsus. But

I hear God is really moving in Antioch. I'm only a short boat ride away. If you need any help . . ." No, Saul was content to stay in Tarsus plowing through hard ground. Faithful to the task in front of him, he waited for God's timing. Then his old advocate Barnabas tapped him on the shoulder and said, "We need you in Antioch. Can you come?" And, after seven or eight years of being shaped, tooled, and polished in a manner few today would welcome or embrace, he was ready.

> And for an entire year they met with the church and
> taught considerable numbers; and the disciples were
> first called Christians in Antioch. (v. 26b)

Saul's teaching had come a long way since his days in Jerusalem! There was a remarkable difference because Saul was different—he had been changed within. Under the shadow of the Almighty, he had been humbled. He was a new man. One who died to self and put no confidence in the flesh. One who relied more on his God than his gifts. One who learned dependence through years of obscurity and countless trials.

Four Principles from the Shadows

We can illuminate four principles from studying Saul's time spent in the shadows. As we relate each one to our lives, we will find a character quality God desires to craft in us.

Principle One: *When God prepares us for effective ministry, He includes what we would rather omit—a period of waiting.* This culti-vates patience in us. Unfortunately, patience lands close to the bottom of our own Top Ten list of character traits. "Hurry" perme-ates our culture. We receive periods of waiting as we do telemarketers—hurry up so I can get on with life. When God forces us to wait, whether for a job, a mate, a child, or a ministry, we usually try to take matters into our own hands. But, in order for us to be perfected in Christ, we must practice patience. James states:

> Consider it all joy, my brethren, when you en-
> counter various trials, knowing that the testing of
> your faith produces endurance. And let endurance
> have its perfect result, so that you may be perfect
> and complete, lacking in nothing. (1:2–4)

Principle Two: *As God makes us wait, hiding us in the shadows, He shows us we are not indispensable.* That makes us humble. If we ever approach ministry with an air of "They'd better be glad they have me" or "This ministry couldn't continue if I didn't lead it," watch out. God's not a talent agent hoping the best and the brightest sign up for His program. He's a master conductor who seamlessly weaves the first chair violin with the third chair flute. Depending on the movement, we may perform a solo heard by all, join with the rest for a heart-pounding crescendo, or patiently wait for the tip of His baton. Regardless, it's an honor just to play in His orchestra.

Principle Three: *When God hides us away, He reveals new dimensions of Himself and new insights regarding ministry.* That results in spiritual depth and maturity. How's your devotional life? If you're like most, devotions vie for a spot between the hectic morning and the harried evening. God sequesters us so that we may find Him. Jesus Himself stole away from the masses by ascending the mountains. When God sends us to the desert of obscurity, rather than cursing the sand, let's rest in the oasis of His presence.

Principle Four: *When God finally chooses to use us, it comes at a time least expected, when we feel the least qualified.* That makes us effective. The perfect set-up for a long-lasting, effective ministry begins with surprise. "Oh, me? You sure you don't want the guy next door?" With such an attitude, you join the ranks of Abraham, Moses, David, Esther, Peter, and Saul, people God used to accomplish great things as they responded to Him with humility and obedience.

Living in the Light

> Be not afraid to trust God utterly. As you go down the long corridor you may find that He has preceded you and locked many doors which you would fain have entered; but be sure that beyond these there is one which He has left unlocked. Open it and enter— and you will find yourself face to face with a bend of the river of opportunity, broader and deeper than anything you had dared to imagine. . . . Launch forth on it; it conducts to the open sea.[4]

---

4. James Swanson, *A Dictionary of Biblical Languages with Semantic Domains: Hebrew* (Old Testament), 2d ed. (published electronically: Logos Research Systems Inc., 2001), accessed through the Logos Library System.

Propelled by impatience, pride, and insecurity, we often try to break the locks with the crowbar of self-will. We feel we've waited long enough. We may be able to get through the door, but we'll never be satisfied with what's inside. God will show you the way— even if it leads you through the shadows—and He will accomplish the exceptional through you. Who knows, someone may be guessing your name before Paul Harvey utters those immortal words, "Now you know the rest of the story."

Living Insights

What keeps you up at night? Just as your eyelids begin their descent, what thoughts dart in front of them and act as a doorstop to sleep? Is it a bill that you know won't be paid? Is it the thought that you may never find the right person to marry? Could it be a longing for the salvation of your ill father?

Whatever the issue, you're not alone. Minute by minute people wage war between confidently waiting and incessantly worrying. The word used in the Bible for *wait* can be translated, "look forward with confidence to that which is good and beneficial, often with a focus of anticipation in a future event." How do we "look forward with confidence" amidst a tornado of stress and anxiety?

Take a page out of David's struggles:

> Teach me Your way, O Lord,
> And lead me in a level path
> Because of my foes.
>
> Do not deliver me over to the desire of my
> adversaries,
> For false witnesses have risen against me,
> And such as breathe out violence.
>
> I would have despaired unless I had believed that I
> would see the goodness of the Lord
> In the land of the living.
>
> Wait for the Lord;
> Be strong and let your heart take courage;
> Yes, wait for the Lord. (Psalm 27:11–14)

From David, we can learn principles for dealing with pressure.

49

Admit Your Inadequacy

The temptation is to live in denial. We want desperately to have it all together. But that's where God wants to meet us—in our weakness, in our struggles, and in our pain.

Press On

Continue to live life, work hard, and deepen your relationships with others. We're not in God's waiting room, wringing our hands and hoping He will send a remedy so we can move on with our lives. He will act *amidst* our struggles.

Trust in the Future because of the Past

David remembered God's goodness in the past, which gave him confidence God would act in the future. Even if you choose not to acknowledge it, God has a perfect track record in your life. He delivered you before; He'll deliver you again. When anxiety floods your heart, latch onto His past provision. We often wait by worrying; God asks us to wait by trusting.

On the lines below, briefly describe times in your life when God has come through for you. Then write down any attributes or promises of God that come to mind.

_____

_____

_____

_____

_____

_____

_____

_____

Remember, God is unchanging, and He keeps His promises. He says in His Word: "I will never leave you nor forsake you." Bow your head in prayer now; recommit yourself to waiting in hopeful expectation for God's purposes to be fulfilled.

 *Questions for Group Discussion*

1. In what ways does our culture encourage us to be impatient and frantically busy? How does this affect your daily life and your schedule? What impact does this have on your walk with God?

2. Name a time when you had to wait on God. What were the circumstances? What happened as a result? How did this period of waiting strengthen your faith?

3. What results does patience accomplish in our Christian lives? Take time to look up verses in the Bible that discuss patience, waiting, and endurance. Why is it so important that Christians cultivate these qualities?

4. Do you feel like you are waiting for God's direction and His answers in certain areas of your life right now? If so, what are these areas? How can you spend this time "looking forward with confidence" to the results of the work that God is doing in your life?

5. If you have just come through a time of waiting, how can you use your experience to encourage others in the group who may be facing hard times?

Chapter 7

FINDING CONTENTMENT IN GOD'S SUFFICIENT GRACE

2 Corinthians 12:1–10

G od loves you and offers a wonderful plan for your life."[1] These are words that ring true to us in days of blessing but hang hollow in seasons of suffering. If it's such a "wonderful life," why doesn't the movie starring you share the Jimmy-Stewart ending? In your life's movie, cancer conquers your loved one. The company downsizes you. Friends fade. Despite your prayers, it seems as if God doesn't deliver.

Take heart. You are in good company, joining the ranks of all Christians and even the superstar servant known as the apostle Paul. In the most autobiographical of his letters, 2 Corinthians, Paul revealed how he struggled against affliction as he walked through his own "wonderful life" filled with pain, persecution, and power.

Paul's Perspective

Saul, a murderer of missionaries, turned missionary himself when he met Jesus in a blinding light on the road to Damascus (Acts 9:3–6). Later in his ministry, he was renamed Paul and again encountered God face-to-face. He recounted this trip to paradise in 2 Corinthians 12:1–6. He prefaced his story with:

> Boasting is necessary, though it is not profitable;
> but I will go on to visions and revelations of the
> Lord. (v. 1)

Paul addressed boasting because, in his day, false apostles promoted their own agendas, leading the Corinthians astray. They spoke false words about God that caused some of the people to follow incorrect human ideas rather than God's truth. Paul believed that trusting the Lord's truth rather than human ideas authenticated the message of Christ. He desired the Corinthians to exalt the true God rather than to esteem false prophets. When Paul spoke of the

---

1. *The Four Spiritual Laws*, available at http://www.fourspirituallaws.com/laws/English, accessed November 14, 2002.

vision, he focused on God's power as the Revealer rather than on himself as the receiver of the revelation.

Paul's Privilege

Paul continued:

> I know a man in Christ who fourteen years ago—whether in the body I do not know, or out of the body I do not know, God knows—such a man was caught up to the third heaven. And I know how such a man—whether in the body or apart from the body I do not know, God knows—was caught up into Paradise and heard inexpressible words, which a man is not permitted to speak. (vv. 2–4)

Paul knew about the man "caught up to the third heaven" because the man was Paul himself. He dated the event. He described where it occurred. He detailed what happened in a way that only an eyewitness could. While clear on his location—"the third heaven,"[2] he was fuzzy about his embodiment. The presence of God so consumed Paul that it eclipsed his awareness of the physical world of space and time so that he did not know whether he was in or out of his body. Possibly, Paul ascended to the third heaven in his earthly body. Or he might have had an out-of-body experience in which his spirit traveled to paradise without his earthly body.

The Greek word for "caught up," *harpazo*, denotes rapture.[3] First Thessalonians 4:17 uses the same word when it describes Christ's return—when Christians "will be caught up . . . in the clouds to meet the Lord in the air." The chief difference between Paul's *harpazo* in 2 Corinthians 12:2 and the one mentioned in 1 Thessalonians 4:17 lies in the fact that Paul witnessed the Lord's presence in the third heaven and *returned* to earth. No other apostle got a round-trip ticket to heaven! In an instant, Paul, an earth-dweller like his fellow disciples, exited this world, beamed to heaven, and returned home to tell the others about his celestial excursion.

---

2. Jesus and the people who had followed God on earth before they died dwelled in the third heaven, or paradise, as Jesus referred to it.

3. William F. Arndt and F. Wilbur Gingrich, eds., *A Greek-English Lexicon of the New Testament and Other Early Christian Literature*, 2d ed. (Chicago, Ill.: The University of Chicago Press, 1979), p. 109.

Though Paul grasped what God revealed to him during this experience, he could not fully express it to others. Though God's message fortified Paul for future suffering and service, its delivery defied words. For a moment, put yourself in Paul's sandals. Once blinded and knocked to the ground in the glare of Jesus' glory, then snatched from this earth—in or out of your skin—to behold the face of God. Paul's debut in Damascus was amazing; his presence in paradise was awe striking.

Paul's Potential Pride

Imagine the bragging rights!

> "Hey, Peter, have *you* jetted to heaven lately?"

> "Matthew, if you think the vista from the Mount of Olives takes your breath away, you should catch the view from paradise."

> "Oh, that's right, James, you haven't seen Jesus since the Day of Pentecost. He didn't invite *you* to His mansion."

The potential for spiritual conceit abounded, but Paul was determined to continue living his life depending on the Lord for his contentment and self-worth. He refused to be like the guy born on third base who thought he'd hit a triple. This expression describes a person born into privilege who prides himself on his high standing though he did nothing to earn it. In contrast, Paul lavished the praise on the source of his strength, Christ. He wrote:

> On behalf of such a man I will boast; but on my own behalf I will not boast, except in regard to my weaknesses. For if I do wish to boast I will not be foolish, for I will be speaking the truth; but I refrain from this, so that no one will credit me with more than he sees in me or hears from me. (2 Cor. 12:5–6)

Unlike the person "born on third base," Paul saw the foolishness of having confidence in his own strength and ability. He recognized that all the noteworthy acts that he did and the memorable words that he spoke came from the Lord. He humbly acknowledged his weakness.

54

Paul's Pain

After recounting the privilege of joining Jesus in person, Paul presented the pain of his weakness:

> Because of the surpassing greatness of the revelations, for this reason, to keep me from exalting myself, there was given me a thorn in the flesh, a messenger of Satan to torment me—to keep me from exalting myself! (v. 7)

God gave Paul a thorn in the flesh to pierce his pride. The Greek word for thorn, *skolops*, denotes a pointed stake used as an "injurious foreign body."[4] On the heels of privilege came throbbing pain. In Eugene Peterson's modern paraphrase, *The Message*, Paul calls this thorn a gift:

> Because of the extravagance of those revelations, and so I wouldn't get a big head, I was given the *gift* of a handicap to keep me in constant touch with my limitations. Satan's angel did his best to get me down; what he in fact did was push me to my knees. No danger then of walking around high and mighty! (v. 7 THE MESSAGE, emphasis added)[5]

God granted Paul the thorn to keep him from being arrogant, from boasting about the greatness of receiving God's revelation. And he lived with the thorn's nagging effects for the rest of his life. Speculation about the specific nature of Paul's affliction runs the gamut. Some suggest spiritual temptations while others postulate carnal cravings. Still more claim it was opposition and persecution, physical deformity, epilepsy, migraines, serious eye trouble, a hunchback, or virulent malarial fever. The true culprit is unknown.

Paul called the thorn a "messenger of Satan" because the Enemy hoped to use it to thwart his mission. But the Lord purposely allowed it in order to bring Paul to his knees in weakness. While Satan punched and pounded Paul, the Father fortified him. According to Lenski, a respected theologian, "The higher Paul's work was, the more he needed humility. The more divine his work was, the more

---

4. Arndt and Gingrich, A *Greek-English Lexicon*, p. 756.

5. Eugene H. Peterson, *The Message: The Bible in Contemporary Language* (Colorado Springs, Colo.: NavPress, 2002), p. 294.

necessary for him was the constant realization of utter dependence on the Lord; for if [the Lord] withdraws his hand, Satan would have [Paul] utterly in his power."[6]

How can this be? Surely God wouldn't humiliate His people. Wouldn't our earthly grandeur better reflect His glory? After all, He does promise success to the saints, right? Wrong. The ancient book of Job argues differently when it says, "For man is born for trouble/As sparks fly upward" (Job 5:7). Job, a man chosen to suffer, recognized that we should receive both good things and trials from God with open hands. Both bless us. God's good comforts us, and His trials challenge us to mature into Christlikeness.

Paul's Petition

Initially, Paul hated his handicap and begged God for relief:

> Concerning this I implored the Lord three times that it might leave me. (2 Cor. 12:8)

Three times he petitioned. Three times God provided the same answer: No. He didn't say "wait." He never offered "maybe." He stuck with the solid "N-O." Why? Because it rooted Paul more deeply in God. Often God's will does not include physical or emotional healing. Sometimes He lets the pressure build to accomplish His greatest goal of making His children more dependent on Him.

God's Gift

According to *The Message*, Paul's view of the thorn began to change.

> At first I didn't think of it as a gift, and begged God to remove it. Three times I did that, and then he told me, "My grace is enough; it's all you need. My strength comes into its own in your weakness." Once I heard that, I was glad to let it happen. I quit focusing on the handicap and began appreciating the gift. It was a case of Christ's strength moving in on my weakness. Now I take limitations in stride, and with good cheer, these limitations that cut me

6. R. C. H. Lenski, *The Interpretation of St. Paul's First and Second Epistles to the Corinthians* (Minneapolis, Minn.: Augsburg Publishing House, 1961), p. 1301.

down to size—abuse, accidents, opposition, bad
breaks. I just let Christ take over! And so the weaker
I get, the stronger I become. (vv. 8–10 THE MESSAGE)[7]

Paul shifted his focus from the object of his affliction to the
person of his praise. He discovered that God would not provide
healing, but He would shower sufficient grace. God promised Paul
that divine grace would give him the strength to persevere through
his pain. God perfects His children in their human weakness.

God's Glory

And He has said to me, "My grace is sufficient for
you, for power is perfected in weakness." Most gladly,
therefore, I will rather boast about my weaknesses,
so that the power of Christ may dwell in me. (v. 9)

Paul experienced contentment because he realized that the Lord
gave him strength when he felt weak. He knew that God provided
him the power to press on when he reached the end of himself. He
bragged only in God because God sustained him when his own
resources failed.

Therefore I am well content with weaknesses, with
insults, with distresses, with persecutions, with difficulties, for Christ's sake; for when I am weak, then
I am strong. (v. 10)

When we rely on our own strength, we get the credit, but we
keep going independently of Christ. When we admit our inability
to do it alone, He steps to the forefront and carries us. We give
Him the praise for our success because He makes it happen.

Don't forget that the very things we try to escape are the things
He wants us to bring to Him so that He can help us. Look at Paul's
list: I am content when I lose. I am content when I am weak. I am
content with insults. I am content when I'm slandered. I am content
in distresses. I am content with persecutions. I am content with
difficulties and pressures that are so tight I can hardly turn around.
I AM CONTENT. Why? Because in my weakness, His strength
shines. What a way to live your life—content in everything—
knowing that divine strength comes when human weakness is evident.

7. Peterson, The Message, p. 294.

That's what gave the man of grace true grit. It will do the same for us if we remember our suffering is not new, if we realize that suffering brings us closer to our Lord, and if we release the idea that contentment requires comfort. We can experience contentment no matter how dire our situation. Years later, while under house arrest, Paul wrote, "I have learned to be content in whatever circumstances I am. I know how to get along with humble means, and I also know how to live in prosperity; in any and every circumstance I have learned the secret of being filled and going hungry, both of having abundance and suffering need. I can do all things through Him who strengthens me" (Phil. 4:11–13). He said it again! The secret to Paul's contentment was his certainty that Christ's strength perfected his weakness.

God's Grace Is Sufficient for Our Lives Today

We live in shallow, skeptical times. When hard times hit, critics accuse God of injustice. According to Philip Yancey, they "assume that the amount of evil and suffering in this world cannot be matched with the traditional view of a good and loving God. Therefore, many of them adjust their conception of God, either redefining His love or questioning His power to control evil."[8] The next time suffering socks you, will you, like Paul, plant your feet firmly on the ground and face your foe, embracing your grief as a God-given gift? Or will you run with the crowd, missing the box of contentment wrapped in the paper of pain?

Not only is God's grace sufficient, His power will show more brightly through human weakness. It turns out that the superstar of Paul's movie—and ours, too—is God. Your life's not a B-rated flop at all. It's a blockbuster! You just had the main player miscast. The plot revolves not around you and your pain, but around God's perfect plan. We get the applause when we keep going in our own strength. He receives the standing ovation when He carries us in our weakness. Never forget, God is the star. We are the supporting cast.

8. Philip Yancey, *Where Is God When It Hurts?* (Grand Rapids, Mich.: Zondervan Publishing House, 1977), p. 84.

Living Insights

Read Hebrews 12:9–11 and answer the questions that follow.

Why does God discipline us? _____

_____

How do we tend to respond? _____

_____

What fruit does discipline yield? _____

_____

How does discipline strengthen us spiritually? _____

_____ –

Are you struggling with a thorn or painful experience? Are you, like Paul, begging God to remove it and He keeps saying no? Take time now to humble yourself before God, acknowledging Him as sovereign and recognizing your own inability to handle it alone.

Write a brief description of your situation below. List any feelings and circumstances that you need to relinquish to God's control. Think of stubborn sins that need confessing. After you finish writing, go to the Lord in prayer about these things. He is ready to embrace you and sustain you by His grace.

_____ –

_____

_____

_____

_____

_____

_____

_____

_____

_____

_____

God loves us so deeply that He disciplines us to strengthen our spiritual limbs. He desires us to see Him as our sun and shield, as did the psalmist in Psalm 84:11. Run to Him for comfort and protection, and you will find contentment. Walk uprightly and revel in His good things.

 *Questions for Group Discussion*

1. What lessons did God teach Paul through suffering?

2. Our society suggests two aspirins for every headache, offers plastic surgery for a not-so-young face, and promises certain love in a bottle of perfume. An answer for every problem. A quick fix to stop the pain. In what ways do we tend to look for the quick fix to avoid pain? Why?

3. What unexpected blessings have you gained in your life from painful experiences? How did God change your heart through these past experiences?

4. Think about a difficult issue in your life right now. In light of your reflections on Paul's suffering, share your perspective of your struggle with the group. How is God using this issue to work in your life?

Chapter 8

THE PLEASURE OF BEING IN MINISTRY TOGETHER

Acts 11:21–30; 12:24–25

Someone once asked Leonard Bernstein, the late composer and famed conductor of the world-renowned New York Philharmonic, what he believed to be the most difficult instrument in the orchestra to play. He replied, "Second fiddle!"[1]

We all know how tough it can be to "play second fiddle." But we also know how much our success depends on encouragement and support from our loved ones. When you take time to examine the lives of great individuals, you'll see that each of them had support from loving people behind the scenes who never asked for glory or recognition. These people were content to serve humbly and let others receive the credit.

Some of the greatest biblical relationships reflected this dynamic—Moses and Aaron, David and Jonathan, Ruth and Naomi, Esther and Mordecai, Elijah and Elisha. This leader/supporter pattern has continued through the centuries as God has raised up faithful men and women to edify His people and spread His Word.

God has a way of banding together remarkably different persons for the most marvelous of enterprises—the mission of sharing the Good News of Christ. In His grace, the Lord designed that we would serve Him not in *isolation*, but in *relationship*. Acts 11:21–30 outlines the formation of a dynamic partnership between Saul and Barnabas. Their moving example illustrates how much fruit we can reap when we minister in close relationship with one another.

An Overwhelming Task Ahead

God called His dream team, Paul and Barnabas, to minister to those who came to Christ during a great revival. This revival occurred in Antioch—the most unexpected of places. Antioch represented a first-century "sin city" notorious for its gambling, idol

---

1. Leonard Bernstein, as quoted by Charles R. Swindoll in *Paul: A Man of Grace and Grit* (Nashville, Tenn.: The W Publishing Group, 2002), p. 109.

worship, and sexual immorality. Many would have written off the city as a hopeless spiritual wasteland . . . but not God. He had other plans.

Verses 19–20 of Acts 11 reveal how the Lord worked through these two men in Antioch:

> So then those who were scattered because of the persecution that arose in connection with Stephen made their way to Phoenicia and Cyprus and Antioch, speaking the word to no one except to Jews alone. But there were some of them, men of Cyprus and Cyrene, who came to Antioch and began speaking to the Greeks also, preaching the Lord Jesus.

Verse 19 refers to the events recorded in Acts 7, which culminated in the death of the first Christian martyr, Stephen. Yet instead of hindering the spread of the Gospel, this milestone event provided a means for Christians to share the Good News. Because of the persecution associated with this tragedy, believers traveled to new regions to plant the message of Christ, and even Gentiles were beginning to hear it. The Lord abundantly blessed the ministry of those who shared the Gospel:

> And the hand of the Lord was with them, and a large number who believed turned to the Lord. (11:21)

Imagine living in Antioch—a metropolis of indulgence, barren of truth, full of pagan rituals and idol worship. Then suddenly, *revival!* So great was the harvest of souls that word spread quickly, and "the news about them reached the ears of the church at Jerusalem" (v. 22a).

When the Christian leaders in Jerusalem heard this marvelous report, they acted quickly. They recognized that a spiritual awakening of this magnitude required careful shepherding by a well-qualified person. So, trusting Barnabas's wisdom and experience, "they sent Barnabas off to Antioch" (v. 22b).

Barnabas was nicknamed by the apostles "Son of Encouragement" (Acts 4:36). His name could also be translated "Son of Consolation."[2] The verb *console* means "to alleviate the grief, sense

---

2. William F. Arndt and F. Wilbur Gingrich, eds., *A Greek-English Lexicon of the New Testament and Other Early Christian Literature*, 2d ed. (Chicago, Ill.: The University of Chicago Press, 1979), p. 133.

of loss, or trouble of; to comfort."[3] As a gifted encourager, Barnabas was the perfect choice to minister to the quickly growing congregation in Antioch:

> Then when he arrived and witnessed the grace of God, he rejoiced and began to encourage them all with resolute heart to remain true to the Lord; for he was a good man, and full of the Holy Spirit and of faith. And considerable numbers were brought to the Lord. (11:23–24)

Notably, Barnabas didn't encourage the people with only kind words and a hearty pat on the back. He specifically encouraged them "with resolute heart to remain true to the Lord" (v. 23). Barnabas was not simply a gifted people-person; he was a man of faith, one who knew the value of discipleship. He longed to see these new children of God grow stronger in their knowledge of and commitment to Christ.

As Barnabas's uplifting ministry continued, the Spirit continued to move, and considerable numbers of new believers came to faith in the Lord (v. 24b). Barnabas realized he needed some help, and he knew exactly where to turn. He longed for someone to assist him in shepherding this new flock, and it had to be someone who could ground them in solid doctrine. So, as we learned in chapter 6, "he left for Tarsus to look for Saul" (v. 25).

The Remarkable Power of Two

Saul (who would come to be known as Paul)[4] would no doubt be a valuable asset to this developing community of faith. While Barnabas was legendary for his encouraging spirit, Saul had quite a reputation for his doctrinal depth and ardent contention for the truth. Moreover, since Barnabas's last encounter with him, Saul had certainly met with his share of amazing and powerfully formative experiences.

---

3. *Merriam-Webster's Collegiate Dictionary*, 10th ed., see "console."

4. The name change (from 13:9 to the end of Acts, as well as in all of Paul's letters) from the Hebrew name "Saul" to the Roman name "Paul" probably represents a deliberate focus on the new audience to which the apostle would direct his ministry for the rest of his life, the Gentile community. See Kenneth O. Gangel, *Acts: Holman New Testament Commentary*, ed. Max Anders (Nashville, Tenn.: Broadman & Holman, 1998), p. 213.

In the seven or eight years since these two had parted, suffering for Christ had become a lifestyle for Saul. He had narrowly escaped assassination in Damascus (9:23–25), wrestled with the "thorn in the flesh" given him by the Lord (2 Cor. 12:7–8), and been disowned, not only by the Pharisees and other religious leaders, but most likely by his family as well. Refined in the fire of these struggles, Paul wrote to the Corinthians, "Therefore I am well content with weaknesses, with insults, with distresses, with persecutions, with difficulties, for Christ's sake; for when I am weak, then I am strong" (v. 10).

During this time, the Lord had been preparing Saul for a lifetime of ministry. Saul had been forged into a man of faith, maturity, and unparalleled character. With Barnabas at his side to encourage and assist him, this apostle would grow to become one of the most influential men in the history of the church. Yet Saul wasn't out campaigning for apostleship or advertising his gifts. Instead, Barnabas sought him out and brought him to Antioch. Saul possessed a humble willingness to serve rather than selfish ambition.

A Ministry Team Is Born

After all the years of affliction and triumph, who appeared on Saul's doorstep? Barnabas. The very man who had introduced and commended him to the apostles after his conversion (Acts 9:26–27) now sought his assistance. This must have come as something of a surprise for Saul, but he knew well the warm embrace of this friend, and they were soon on the road to greet the church at Antioch:

> And for an entire year they met with the church
> and taught considerable numbers; and the disciples
> were first called Christians in Antioch. (11:26b)

When God uses us to further His kingdom, we reap joy and a feeling of accomplishment. Undoubtedly, this was true for Barnabas and Saul, men so driven by godly zeal and love. They provided the perfect complement to one another—the compassionate encourager and the fervent, systematic teacher. Barnabas and Saul selflessly set aside any competition or hidden agendas, and they counted it a profound privilege to work together. In concert, they formed a uniquely effective ministry team, tailored to the specific needs of this new congregation.

The Fruits of a Team Effort in the Lord

The ministry of these two men reveals another key reason for valuing teamwork: Astonishing results materialize when the Lord takes pleasure in His people working together. In time, Barnabas and Saul saw the payoff for all of their hard labor. They had already witnessed the electrifying work of the Spirit turning people's hearts to Christ, and now God's hand was becoming manifestly evident in their discipleship.

The spiritual growth of the people of Antioch expressed itself in a variety of ways. First of all, *it became evident in their public reputation.* The end of Acts 11:26 declares that "the disciples were first called Christians in Antioch." The word *Christian* marked people as Christ's servants.[5] Commentator Kenneth Gangel notes that the term was an "outside nickname, possibly given in derision."[6] Of course, for those who love Christ, this term is no insult, but a label His followers have cherished for over two thousand years. What a testimony to the lives of these new believers at Antioch that their neighbors would consider their defining trait to be their service to the Lord Jesus!

The second evidence of spiritual growth that Barnabas and Saul witnessed in the believers at Antioch was *an uncommon generosity.* When a crisis arose, this thriving community responded in an extraordinarily loving manner:

> Now at this time some prophets came down from Jerusalem to Antioch. One of them named Agabus stood up and began to indicate by the Spirit that there would certainly be a great famine all over the world. And this took place in the reign of Claudius. And in the proportion that any of the disciples had means, each of them determined to send a contribution for the relief of the brethren living in Judea. And this they did, sending it in charge of Barnabas and Saul to the elders. (Acts 11:27–30)

True faith reveals itself in action, especially love, and the Christians of Antioch displayed this in abundance. When a severe famine

---

5. F. F. Bruce, *New Testament History* (Garden City, N.J.: Doubleday, 1972), p. 267.

6. Gangel, *Acts,* p. 181.

befell the land, these new disciples were deeply moved by the plight of Christians living back in Judea. They disregarded their own needs for the sake of their distant brothers and sisters, sending a relief offering. It must have been immensely fulfilling for Barnabas and Saul to return to the Judean leaders with tangible validation of the love and devotion of those they had discipled. The two ministers had been a part of a great revival in which the Lord had graciously brought them together and used them for His glory, the very passion and purpose of their lives.

Acts 12:24–25 provides an epilogue on the lasting results of the mighty efforts of this team. Spurred on through this and, no doubt, other mission endeavors,

> the word of the Lord continued to grow and to be multiplied. And Barnabas and Saul returned from Jerusalem when they had fulfilled their mission, taking along with them John, who was also called Mark.

With the church flourishing and the Gospel continuing to spread, Barnabas and Saul returned to their ministry in Antioch. Along the way, they picked up a new recruit, the young John Mark. Together, this godly trio set out to shepherd souls.

Timeless Essentials for Ministering Together

Just as God called Barnabas and Saul, He also calls us. While He may not expect you to do the same job as one of these two men, you do play a part in fulfilling His Great Commission. As Paul later wrote, "For we are His workmanship, created in Christ Jesus for good works, which God prepared beforehand so that we would walk in them" (Eph. 2:10).

Every ministry needs at least three essential perspectives in order to produce an atmosphere of joyful cooperation. First, *whatever God plans, He pursues*. God empowers us to be engaged in ministry, but we're never indispensable. He will use our prayers and wise decision-making, but this is His work. And His work always involves surprises. As you follow the Spirit's leading in your life, you will be amazed at the creativity of our God in how He chooses to bring honor to His name.

Second, *whomever God chooses, He uses*. Even though the Lord is fully capable of working apart from people, He takes pleasure in working through us. What's more, He is especially pleased to use us corporately to fulfill His purposes. Paul illustrates this beautifully in the book of 1 Corinthians:

> But to each one is given the manifestation of the Spirit for the common good. . . . For even as the body is one and yet has many members, and all the members of the body, though they are many, are one body, so also is Christ. (1 Cor. 12:7, 12)

Third, *wherever God selects, He sends.* When God unites the purposes of His plan with the people of His choosing, He sets His people in the places He desires. The remarkable revival of Antioch warns us against writing off any location or people group as unreachable. The Lord will work where He wants, when He wants. Our responsibility is simply to join together with the partners He has given us and follow His calling in humble obedience.

The Lord purposely designed the work of ministry so that we, His people, depend on one another. He may choose certain individuals to perform more visible works, but each of these individuals depends greatly on the people God has placed around them. We may someday be called to be the one in the limelight, or we may not. But as we cultivate humility and learn to support and encourage each other, we'll discover how to "play second fiddle" with grace.

Living Insights

One of the highlights of serving together as a team is seeing people who might otherwise be overlooked take on an active role in ministry. Not everyone will preach, teach, sing, or give large donations, but everyone can do *something.* Paul exhorts us to discover our spiritual gifts and contribute what we can to the body of Christ:

> And the eye cannot say to the hand, "I have no need of you"; or again the head to the feet, "I have no need of you." On the contrary, it is much truer that the members of the body which seem to be weaker are necessary; and those members of the body which we deem less honorable, on these we bestow more abundant honor, and our less presentable members become much more presentable, whereas

our more presentable members have no need of it. But God has so composed the body, giving more abundant honor to that member which lacked, so that there may be no division in the body, but that the members may have the same care for one another. (1 Cor. 12:21–25)

The apostles knew that every gift is useful and important to the health of the church body. They refused to take their leadership status so seriously that others would miss out on the opportunity to exercise their gifts. The perfect example arose when conflict ensued because certain widows were being disregarded in the distribution of food. The apostles knew Christ had entrusted them with the responsibility of the steadfast proclamation of the Gospel, and so they concluded, "It is not desirable for us to neglect the word of God in order to serve tables" (Acts 6:2). Realizing they could not do it all, they decided to make good use of the gifted people around them:

> "Therefore, brethren, select from among you seven men of good reputation, full of the Spirit and of wisdom, whom we may put in charge of this task. But we will devote ourselves to prayer and to the ministry of the word." (vv. 3–4)

With that, godly people full of untapped skills were brought off the bench and onto the field so that all of God's purposes could be carried out for the church. Often the needs of the church are opportunities for including our brothers and sisters in the work of the Lord.

As you look around you, do you recognize the giftedness of fellow believers? If God has promised to give His Spirit to each individual for the good of the whole body, then anytime somebody's unique qualities are left out or overlooked, it's our loss. We *need* everyone's participation.

Take a moment to consider your own church or community of believers. What are the ministry needs that might call for more attention? Do you know someone who might fill these roles well?

_____

_____

_____

_____

_____

Can you think of any members who seem marginalized or whose gifts are underutilized? What are some ways you might be able to include these people in the church's work or encourage them to use their gifts?

_____

_____

_____

_____

What about you? Do you know what spiritual gifts God has given you? For a list of spiritual gifts, see Ephesians 4:7–13 and Romans 12:3–8. Also, consider asking your friends or pastor what qualities they see God bringing out in you. Pray for opportunities to use those gifts for God's glory.

_____

_____

_____

_____

Questions for Group Discussion

1. How do you go about initiating and building relationships with people within your sphere of influence? What can you and the others in your small group do to build closer relationships with one another?

2. What steps can you take to encourage those around you who are hurting? What can you do to meet the real needs of your small group, church, and community?

3. How does God use difficult circumstances to forge humility in our lives? In what ways does the condition of our relationships reflect the condition of our hearts?

4. How can pride and ambition hurt our relationships with one another? What can we do to prevent ourselves from "giving the Devil a foothold" in these areas?

5. What positive results and benefits do you reap as a result of your relationships with other believers? With nonbelievers? With coworkers? With family members?

Chapter 9

RELEASED IN ORDER TO OBEY

Acts 13:1–5, 13

Scottish writer A. J. Cronin once wrote,

> Life is no straight and easy corridor along which we travel free and unhampered, but a maze of passages, through which we must seek our way, lost and confused, now and again checked in a blind alley.
>
> But always, if we have faith, a door will open for us, not perhaps one that we ourselves would ever have thought of, but one that will ultimately prove good for us.[1]

Sometimes we feel like mice running frantically through life's maze of passages, trying to find some cheese but discovering only dead ends and closed doors. Unwanted changes, painful losses, and disappointing setbacks can cause us to doubt God's goodness. Our inability to discern God's purposes for our future can cause us to question His greater plan.

Clinging to God's Promises

We can be assured deep down that God is working. He reminds us of this truth in Jeremiah 29:11–13:

> "For I know the plans that I have for you," declares the Lord, "plans for welfare and not for calamity to give you a future and a hope. Then you will call upon Me and come and pray to Me, and I will listen to you. You will seek Me and find Me when you search for Me with all your heart."

This chapter has been adapted from "Adjusting to Change," from the Bible study guide *Adventuring with God*, written by Marla Alupoaicei, from the Bible-teaching ministry of Charles R. Swindoll (Plano, Tex.: Insight for Living, 2002).

1. A. J. Cronin, as quoted by Spencer Johnson, M.D., in *Who Moved My Cheese?* (New York, N.Y.: G. P. Putnam's Sons Publishers, 1988), p. 9.

In *The Message*, Eugene Peterson renders the passage this way:

> "I know what I'm doing. I have it all planned out—
> plans to take care of you, not abandon you, plans
> to give you the future you hope for.
>
> When you call on me, when you come and pray
> to me, I'll listen.
>
> When you come looking for me, you'll find me.
>
> Yes, when you get serious about finding me and
> want it more than anything else, I'll make sure you
> won't be disappointed." (vv. 11–13 THE MESSAGE)[2]

Our loving heavenly Father has an extraordinary design for our lives. His "plans for welfare and not for calamity" often come about through changes that don't seem so good at the time, yet we must cling to the promise that God won't abandon us. He offers us a future full of hopeful expectation. He promises that when we truly seek Him, we'll find Him.

Obedience to God requires openness to His plan, and that means openness to change. The dictionary defines the verb *change* as "to make different in some particular."[3] Change is one of life's rare certainties! When our circumstances change, we change. We aren't exactly the same people we were last week, and we won't be exactly the same next week, either. With each day, we grow in faith, knowledge, and experience.

Stepping Out in Faith

We welcome some changes, but we tend to agonize over others. The early Christian leaders also struggled to adjust to change. Acts 13:1–4 tells the story of a difficult turn of events in the lives of several men who had formed close bonds as they ministered together:

> Now there were at Antioch, in the church that
> was there, prophets and teachers: Barnabas, and
> Simeon who was called Niger, and Lucius of Cyrene,
> and Manaen who had been brought up with Herod
> the tetrarch, and Saul. (Acts 13:1)

2. Eugene H. Peterson, *The Message: The Bible in Contemporary Language* (Colorado Springs, Colo.: NavPress, 2002), p. 1413.

3. *Merriam-Webster's Collegiate Dictionary*, 10th ed., see "change."

These five men worked as a band of brothers in the faith, bound by their commitment to God and their zeal to share the Gospel message. As church leaders, Saul and the others had the responsibility of guarding, instructing, and shepherding their flocks. They were also fast friends. They reclined at dinner together, savoring grilled fish, bread, and fragrant wine. They enjoyed close fellowship and sweet communion as they celebrated the joys and victories of their ministry.

But that wasn't all. These men also wept bitterly over the many griefs, failures, and losses experienced by their faith community. They toiled in the trenches, enduring unfathomable pain and difficulty. They were defamed, belittled, and persecuted. Yet they recognized that their *koinonia*, their common experience of faith in God, involved sharing the physical and emotional hardships of their ministry as well as the joys.

Facing Change

As the apostles ministered together, God abruptly called two of them, Saul and Barnabas, to go in a different direction:

> While they were ministering to the Lord and fasting, the Holy Spirit said, "Set apart for Me Barnabas and Saul for the work to which I have called them." Then, when they had fasted and prayed and laid their hands on them, they sent them away. (vv. 2–3)

Most of us have despaired over changes in our relationships at one time or another. Perhaps your once-loving marriage ended in a bitter divorce. You may have lost a beloved spouse, child, or other family member. Perhaps you've lost your job or you've had to leave a place where you felt at home. Maybe you're no longer a part of a close church family due to a move or a church split. Perhaps you miss spending time with a particular best friend or group of friends. If so, you know the feelings of pain, loss, and discouragement that come when something great ends.

The good news is that even in these hard times, God loves you deeply. No matter how terrible a situation may seem, God can use it for good in your life. When you experience difficulty in your relationships, remember this powerful promise:

> And we know that God causes all things to work together for good to those who love God, to those

who are called according to His purpose. (Rom. 8:28)

Every event has a purpose. Our joys remind us of God's greatness, and our losses remind us of our dependency on Him. The Lord uses life's difficulties to cultivate maturity within us and to conform us to the image of Christ:

> For those whom He foreknew, He also predestined
> to become conformed to the image of His Son.
> (Rom. 8:29)

Saul, Barnabas, and the others knew that following God often meant taking leaps of faith into unknown territory. They knew that being conformed to Christ's image meant giving up their own plans and their own rights at times. So Barnabas and Saul obediently responded in faith:

> So, being sent out by the Holy Spirit, they went
> down to Seleucia and from there they sailed to Cyprus.
> (Acts 13:4)

God had changed these men's lives, and now He was changing their plans! He called Saul and Barnabas to follow His directives in order to achieve *His* specific purposes, and they followed:

> When they reached Salamis, they began to proclaim
> the word of God in the synagogues of the Jews; and
> they also had John as their helper. (v. 5)

Undergoing Transformation

We all begin like caterpillars—sluggishly inching forward on a tree branch, stopping once in a while to nibble on the edge of a leaf, then slowly moving forward again. In our caterpillar state, we have no idea that another world awaits us. But then God envelops us with a cocoon of love. When we awaken, we discover that we have become a new, glorious creature. We're transformed! But we can't experience all God has to offer us until we unfurl our wings and take that first invigorating flight into the great unknown.

Paul referred to this extraordinary transformation in Romans 12:2:

> And do not be conformed to this world, but be
> transformed by the renewing of your mind, so that
> you may prove what the will of God is, that which
> is good and acceptable and perfect.

74

Note that we're not transformed so we can follow any path we want! We're transformed so that we may follow the path that God has established for us—that of His good, acceptable, and perfect will. We're changed so we can change others. Harry Emerson Fosdick wrote, "Christians are supposed not merely to endure change, nor even to profit by it, but to *cause* it" (emphasis added).[4]

Not only do we *undergo* a radical change when we establish a relationship with Christ, we should *cause* a radical change! We're His messengers, chosen to take the Good News of Christ to the lost. Instead of simply sighing and accepting the values that the world hands us, we're called to be mature, power-filled, and faithful agents of change.

Isn't it interesting how God uses the most difficult and traumatic experiences of our lives to make us more Christlike? When we fumble and fail, we're humbled. We become more teachable. We seek God's will through prayer. We read His Word. We admit that we're not perfect, and we realize how dependent we are on God for every breath and every step.

Paul and Barnabas realized this firsthand when their ministry project took another unexpected turn. Their traveling companion, John Mark, bailed out on them in the middle of their mission!

> Now Paul and his companions put out to sea from
> Paphos and came to Perga in Pamphylia; but John
> left them and returned to Jerusalem. (Acts 13:13)

Not only were Saul and Barnabas removed from their band of brothers, but their friend John Mark also deserted them on their journey. Yet they faithfully forged ahead, keeping their eyes on the goal and trusting God to lead them. Although they may have wondered about God's plan, they soon realized that He was simply pruning their lives so they would bear more fruit for His kingdom.

Pruning Versus Discipline

Pruning is distinct from *discipline*. The difference between discipline and pruning lies in their causes. Discipline results when we do something wrong, but pruning occurs when we're doing something right! Discipline involves painful correction as a means to restore the wayward believer to the right path of fellowship with the Lord.

---

4. Harry Emerson Fosdick, at http://www.brainyquote.com, accessed on October 24, 2002.

It's important to understand that the pain and suffering caused by God's discipline are not ends in themselves. Rather, our heavenly Father's discipline brings about change in our lives, shapes our character, and brings us back into a loving relationship with Him (see Heb. 12:4–11).

When we grow lackluster or unfruitful due to sin, God disciplines us so that we may again bear fruit. King David understood the negative changes and consequences that could happen in a person's life due to sin. Some time after he committed adultery with Bathsheba and ordered the murder of her husband, Uriah, David finally cried out to God for mercy. He implored God:

> Create in me a clean heart, O God,
> And renew a steadfast spirit within me.
> Do not cast me away from Your presence
> And do not take Your Holy Spirit from me.
> Restore to me the joy of Your salvation
> And sustain me with a willing spirit.
> Then I will teach transgressors Your ways,
> And sinners will be converted to You.
> (Ps. 51:10–13)[5]

God designed disciplinary measures to give believers an opportunity to repent and turn away from their sin in order that they might be restored to fellowship with Him. David experienced severe discipline as a result of his sin, but God eventually restored him.

In contrast with King David, Paul and Barnabas experienced God's *pruning* as He sent them out to minister in the midst of great hardships. These men had certain goals for their ministry, but God, the Great Change Agent, had other ideas! He reshaped their lives. He called them to a new obedience that challenged their faith and left them asking, "Why?" As we bear fruit, God prunes the vines of our lives to allow us to be even more fruitful and productive. He brings change into our lives so that we will depend on Him. He prunes us so we will learn to trust Him and to accept the work He wants to do in us.

As the creative, loving Potter, God had a plan for His clay. He shaped Paul and Barnabas into vessels to be used for His purposes.

---

5. The subheading of Psalm 51 reads, "A Contrite Sinner's Prayer for Pardon" (NASB). The superscription reads, "For the choir director. A Psalm of David, when Nathan the prophet came to him, after he had gone in to Bathsheba."

The prophet Isaiah vividly illustrated this metaphor of God as the Potter and His people as the clay. Isaiah wrote:

> "Woe to the one who quarrels with his Maker—
> An earthenware vessel among the vessels of earth!
> Will the clay say to the potter, 'What are you doing?'
> Or the thing you are making say, 'He has no hands'?"
> (Isa. 45:9)

He also wrote:

> But now, O Lord, You are our Father,
> We are the clay, and You our potter;
> And all of us are the work of Your hand. (64:8)

God conforms us, shapes us, and molds us to make us more obedient worshipers of Him. One author noted:

> The thorough acquaintance of the potter with both the clay and the vessel that he made from it is used to illustrate God's knowledge of humanity. The power of the potter in molding the clay is used to illustrate the absolute power of God in molding the destinies of men (Rom 9:21). To place one's self as clay in the hands of God, as the potter, is a striking figure of complete trust and surrender (Isa. 64:8).[6]

Instead of tossing us aside as an ugly, good-for-nothing lump of clay, God lovingly picked us up and made an exquisite and priceless vessel out of us. He could have left us there on the shelf, our gifts untapped, our beauty hidden. But He drew us out and recognized our true potential. He changed us to make us who He wanted us to be.

The Gift of Change

Have you ever thought about change as a *gift?* Believe it or not, God offers change as a gift to His children—the ones He loves, the ones He created in His own image, the ones for whom His only beloved Son died. Jesus said:

> "If you then, being evil, know how to give good gifts
> to your children, how much more will your Father

---

6. Merrill F. Unger, *The New Unger's Bible Dictionary*, rev. ed., ed. R. K. Harrison (Chicago, Ill.: Moody Press, 1988), see "Potter" under the heading "Handicrafts."

who is in heaven give what is good to those who ask Him!" (Matt. 7:11)

God gives good gifts. He longs for each of us to be fulfilled, to live a blessed and abundant life in Him. He knows what's best for us. Best of all, no matter what circumstances we face, no matter what occurs in our lives, God never changes! He promises in the book of Malachi:

> "For I, the Lord, do not change. . . . Return to Me, and I will return to you," says the Lord of hosts. (Mal. 3:6–7)

Our Father's love, His power, His knowledge, and His plan are perfect. He promises to be the same yesterday, today, and forever! When the winds of change blow and your ship is tossed about on stormy seas, call out to the One who made you, the One who loves you. He promises to be your anchor in times of trouble.

Living Insights

When asked about one of his exquisite masterpieces, sculptor Michelangelo said, "I saw the angel in the marble and carved until I set him free."[7]

Isn't that similar to the way God views us? We may see only a big, ugly chunk of unfinished rock, but He recognizes the polished masterpiece waiting to emerge. As God chisels away the unneeded material, He shapes us into the people He wants us to be. Finally, the beautiful finished product emerges—ourselves in God's image.

Often, we don't see the big picture, but God does. Although change often seems senseless at the time, it's not.

How do you usually respond to change—do you tend to hold on to "the way things were"?

_____

_____

7. Michelangelo Buonarroti, at http://www.brainyquote.com, accessed on November 8, 2002.

Name a time when you obediently stepped out in faith, even though you couldn't see the big picture. What were the circumstances? What happened as a result?

_____

_____

_____

When God looks at your block of marble, what potential does He see? What gifts does He see lying untapped below the surface?

_____

_____

_____

What can you do to help these gifts and abilities emerge?

_____

_____

_____

Questions for Group Discussion

1. Name a time when you experienced an unwelcome change. What was the situation? How did you deal with it?

2. Have you ever had to give up your own plans or rights in order to follow God's call? If so, how?

3. How do you normally respond to change? What emotions do you usually associate with it?

4. Have you ever experienced the Lord's discipline as a result of sin? Have you experienced pruning so you would bear more fruit? If so, describe the circumstances.

5. Discuss the metaphor of God as the Potter and His children as the clay. What significance does this metaphor have in your spiritual life? How does it affect your view of God and your view of yourself?

Chapter 10

THE JAGGED EDGE OF AUTHENTIC MINISTRY

Selections from Acts 13; 14

It's Academy Awards night. Glamorous actors and actresses step from their stretch limousines onto a lush red carpet, sporting multimillion-dollar jewels and exquisite fashions. Eager fans clamor at the entrance, hoping to catch a glimpse of their favorite star. Journalists and photographers jockey for position, trying to get the best photos for their network. TV viewers around the world sit transfixed as the most beautiful, talented, and famous people in Hollywood gather to honor their own with golden status symbols—thirteen-inch-tall statuettes called Oscars.

Now think about your pastor. Your youth minister. Your missionary friend. Those who sacrifice so much to serve the Lord. Those who make an eternal difference in the lives of others. Who recognizes them for their achievements? When they step onto the scene, where are the red carpets, the lights, the screaming fans, and the photographers?

That's right. The paparazzi are nowhere to be found.

Ministry usually brings with it little fame, few perks, low pay, and no fanfare. Anyone who enters the ministry for recognition or money has clearly chosen the wrong profession! Why? Because authentic ministry has a jagged edge. It involves dreams mixed with reality, joy tempered by heartache, new beginnings and painful transitions, friendships and conflicts, activity and exhaustion. The ultimate focus of an authentic ministry must be serving God while serving people.

The apostle Paul felt all these pressures and more as he ministered throughout Asia Minor. This was his first missionary journey, and it was demanding physically, emotionally, mentally, and spiritually. But through it all, Paul served the Lord and His people, showing us how to be authentic ministers of our Lord Jesus Christ.

Paul's Difficult Journey

Acts 13 and 14 record Paul's first missionary journey. Along with Barnabas and John Mark, Paul launched out with one objective: to proclaim the Gospel of Jesus Christ. Let's revisit the places where Paul took the Good News and note the obstacles he encountered along the way.

Cyprus

The first stop on Paul's journey was the island of Cyprus (13:4b). Once he, Barnabas, and John Mark went ashore, they didn't simply build a bonfire on the beach and wait for the people to come hear their message. Instead, they boldly set out to share the Good News. They spent most of their time preaching in two cities: Salamis, to the east (v. 5), and Paphos, to the west (vv. 6–12).

As they entered Paphos, they encountered a Jewish false prophet and magician named Bar-Jesus, also called Elymas, who tried to prevent the proconsul of Cyprus from placing his faith in Jesus Christ (vv. 6–8). But Paul confronted the magician and announced that Elymas would be punished with blindness for a period of time. As a result of this display of God's power and truth, the proconsul, Sergius Paulus, came safely into Jesus' fold (vv. 9–12).

Empowered by the Spirit and encouraged by His saving work, the apostle took courage and traveled west to the coastal city of Perga in Pamphylia, which is now southern Turkey (v. 13a).

Perga

Danger awaited the trio in this rugged region. Many biblical scholars believe that Paul's "thorn in the flesh" stemmed from malaria or some other coastal illness that he acquired here and that this illness caused a permanent disability of some sort. It's quite possible that Paul was visually impaired as a result of this disease.

It was also here, in this inhospitable setting, that young John Mark abandoned his ministry partners (v. 13b). He had undoubtedly been useful to Paul and Barnabas, sharing their burdens and perhaps carrying some of their baggage for them. But suddenly he left them alone, under pressure, with Paul possibly feeling ill and less able to cope with the challenges of traveling. The two missionaries must have felt crushed under the load of their disappointment—in addition to being tired, hungry, and drained of their spiritual, emotional, and physical energy.

Pisidian Antioch

But Paul and Barnabas pressed on to the city of Pisidian Antioch in the region of Pisidia. Here they met with Jews who were eager to hear their message of forgiveness and justification in Christ. However, when the crowds got too big, some of the Jewish leaders became jealous and slandered Paul. So the apostle took the message of grace to the Gentiles instead, which marked the beginning, here in Pisidian Antioch, of his ministry as ambassador to the Gentiles (vv. 14–51a).

Iconium

After this, the two traveled southeast to Iconium, where they narrowly escaped stoning (13:51b–14:5). They made their way southwest to Lystra and Derbe, also traveling through the country-side (see 14:6–7), but the persecution did not stop. In Lystra, not long after Paul miraculously healed a crippled man, the people started to worship Paul and Barnabas, believing them to be Hermes and Zeus (v. 12). But Paul refused the people's praise and pointed them to the One true God instead (vv. 14–15). Even then, Paul and Barnabas could barely keep the crowds from sacrificing to them (v. 18).

But the people's attitude quickly changed when Jews arrived from Antioch and Iconium to slander Paul and Barnabas. Suddenly, those who had been worshiping the two missionaries as gods now stoned Paul and dragged him out of the city, leaving him for dead (v. 19)! But Paul miraculously recovered, and he and Barnabas went to Derbe and continued undaunted to preach the Good News, winning many disciples to Christ (vv. 20–21a).

Going Home

Following these alternately painful and triumphant events, the apostles backtracked all the way to Pisidian Antioch and then back down to the coastal region of Pamphylia. They sailed across the north-eastern part of the Mediterranean Sea, then back to the harbor at Seleucia. Finally, they arrived home in Antioch (v. 26) and reported "all things that God had done with them." Despite their exhaustion, their pain, and the opposition they had faced, they rejoiced that the Lord had opened the door of faith to the Gentiles (v. 27).

Paul and Barnabas's spiritual lives were stretched as God shaped them to be used for His purposes. Throughout their travels, they received mighty blessings as well as deep and real wounds. They encountered many different, painful angles of the jagged edge of ministry. Their mission required grit, determination, and unshak-able faith.

While ministry has its rewards and delights, it's clearly a calling that cannot be successfully pursued in the flesh. Paul's experience on this first missionary journey provides ample proof of that. Let's study three aspects of Paul's authentic ministry more closely to see how God used him to make a difference.

Paul's Authentic Ministry

First, *Paul's ministry was saturated with the Word of God*. Acts 13 and 14 record many specific references to Paul and Barnabas teaching God's Word. They read and taught the Law and the Prophets to the people. They preached and proclaimed the Good News of Christ, exhorting their listeners to repent and believe in Jesus. They showed themselves to be faithful, diligent students and skilled expounders of Scripture. In this way, Paul and Barnabas demonstrated God's power and authority in their lives.

How deep is your relationship with God? Are you filling your life with His Word and sharing His message with others? Do you spend time with the Lord each day? If not, set aside at least fifteen minutes a day to spend reading Scripture and praying. The challenges of your life require it. Your ministry, your family, your spiritual life, and your relationships depend on it!

Second, *Paul's message emphasized the Gospel to the lost and grace to the saved*. This twofold approach worked amazingly well then, and it still works now. To the lost, we're to present the Gospel in a clear way. Imagine the impact we would have on our communities if each Christian would commit to sharing the Gospel once a week with someone who expresses a need! The other half of this commitment is offering grace to those who believe. We often attempt to please those around us by upholding rules and regulations, maintaining impossible, legalistic demands. What a tragic trap! Yet thousands of us are caught in it. When will we ever learn that grace has set us free?

Paul and Barnabas experienced God's grace and salvation firsthand, and they continually preached about these gifts on their journey. Not only that, but they showed grace in their everyday lives. They never returned evil for evil, but constantly ministered, sacrificed, and forgave. They believed in giving the Gospel and living in grace.

Third, *though the public's reaction was mixed, Paul's response was mature*. When he was invited to speak, he did. When he needed to make firm decisions, he did. When he was refused and rejected, he didn't quit. When he was unrealistically admired and adored, he humbly resisted praise and pointed people to the truth. When he was despised and even stoned, he persevered. When he was with fellow believers, he encouraged and affirmed them. And when he came back home to his church body, he was accountable.

Dream big, but remember that authentic ministry has a jagged edge. It brings a lot of surprises along the way. Be prepared for the twists and turns in life's road by staying in the Word and praying each day, asking God for guidance and wisdom for your journey. Be prepared to offer your testimony of salvation to the lost and your testimony of grace to other believers. And remember the example of Paul, who kept "press[ing] on toward the goal for the prize of the upward call of God in Christ Jesus" (Phil. 3:14).

Living Insights

Paul and Barnabas reaped a great harvest of fruit on their journey, yet they also experienced heartbreaking disappointments and losses as they ministered to others. Let's take time now to reflect on the ministry experiences of these two faithful men. We'll also reflect on our own spiritual journey and how God has used difficulties to change our lives and mature our faith.

How did Paul and Barnabas experience the jagged edge of ministry? What do you think was the most difficult part of their journey? Why?

_____

_____

_____

_____

_____

Why do you think God gave Paul a "thorn in the flesh"? How did this "thorn" change Paul's life and influence his ministry?

_____

_____

_____

_____

_____

_____

Have you ever experienced the "jagged edge of ministry" in your own life? If so, how? What did God teach you through this experience?

_____

_____

_____

_____

Do you have friends or family who have had difficult ministry experiences? If so, how did this affect them?

_____

_____

_____

_____

Do you know anyone who is struggling in a particular area of his or her spiritual life or ministry right now? If so, how can you reach out to him or her?

_____

_____

_____

_____

Questions for Group Discussion

1. What have you learned from this chapter about the perils of ministry? How did Paul and Barnabas demonstrate leadership despite their hardships?

2. Have you experienced the "jagged edge of ministry" in your life? If so, how?

3. Talk about the most difficult trip that you have ever been on. What happened? What did you learn from this experience?

4. What was the most fun or exciting trip you ever took? How did it differ from the previous journey?

Chapter 11
A GAME PLAN FOR FACING EXTREME CIRCUMSTANCES
Acts 13:6–16, 45–46; 14:11–27

In his book *Man's Search for Meaning*, author Viktor Frankl wrote these poignant words:

> We who lived in concentration camps can remember the men who walked through the huts comforting others, giving away their last piece of bread. They may have been few in number, but they offer sufficient proof that everything can be taken from a man but one thing: the last of the human freedoms—to choose one's attitude in any given set of circumstances, to choose one's own way.[1]

Frankl's account of his experience profoundly illustrates that we can't choose our circumstances, but we can choose our response. When we awaken in the morning, we decide on our attitude for that day. Our outlook on life emerges from our understanding of our identity, our mission, and our purpose as believers.

People who have the ability to face unimaginable odds possess at their core at least three vital elements: a clear sense of personal identity, a strong sense of mission, and a deep sense of purpose. These people experience true, deep fulfillment in life. Even in the face of hardship, they know who they are, they understand their mission, and they have a clear sense of God's purposes for their lives. They learn to face challenges head-on, transforming their obstacles into opportunities to grow and mature. They may stumble, but rather than falling down or giving up the fight, people who are fulfilled press on. They persevere with a godly attitude, keeping the end goal in sight.

Paul and Barnabas consistently maintained a godly attitude throughout their missionary journey. The two men faced and overcame countless setbacks and obstacles, yet they stayed focused on

1. Viktor Frankl, *Man's Search for Meaning*, as quoted by Charles R. Swindoll in *Paul: A Man of Grace and Grit* (Nashville, Tenn.: The W Publishing Group, 2002), p. 154.

their goal of preaching the Word of God. They expected hardships and planned their responses ahead of time. The more they obeyed, the more they learned to obey. The more they trusted God, the more they learned to trust Him. When they responded positively to one difficult situation, they were better equipped to respond positively again. In the same way, the more we depend on God and trust Him during the relatively easy times, the better able we are to lean on Him when the road gets incredibly rough.

In the previous chapter, we noted how Paul kept his eyes on the goal, despite his encounters with the jagged edge of ministry. In this chapter, we'll focus in on two more aspects of Paul's ministry. First, *though the public's reaction was mixed, Paul's response was mature.* And second, *Paul never forgot that his ministry was about what God had done, not his own accomplishments.* Let's see how Paul's positive attitude and eternal perspective played out in his response to the extreme circumstances he faced on his first missionary journey.

The Power of a Positive Attitude

Even though the public's reaction to their message was mixed, Paul and Barnabas offered a patient and mature response. How? They kept sight of their vision. They had a clear sense of personal identity. They had a firm grasp of their stated mission. And they knew God's purpose for them: to build a bridge of grace to Gentiles who had never heard the Gospel.

Let's take time now to examine seven examples of Paul's mature response to the circumstances that he and Barnabas met along the way. You'll see his grace and grit—his ministry trademarks—come through loud and clear!

A Mature Response to a Phony Prophet

When Paul needed to be firm, he was. He faced a difficult and unusual situation with confidence:

> When they had gone through the whole island as far as Paphos, they found a magician, a Jewish false prophet whose name was Bar-Jesus, who was with the proconsul, Sergius Paulus, a man of intelligence. This man summoned Barnabas and Saul and sought to hear the word of God. But Elymas the magician (for so his name is translated) was opposing them, seeking to turn the proconsul away from the faith. (Acts 13:6–8)

This magician and false prophet actually had the boldness to call himself Bar-Jesus—"Son of Jesus." He accompanied the Roman official Sergius Paulus, whom Luke described as a "proconsul, a man of intelligence." Sergius Paulus had officially summoned Paul and Barnabas to share the Gospel with him. But this man's shady sidekick, Elymas, did not share the same zeal to hear the truth of God. Rather, he vehemently opposed Paul and Barnabas, "seeking to turn the proconsul away from the faith" (v. 8).

Paul and Barnabas immediately stepped up to the plate. Paul firmly reprimanded Elymas, recognizing that the magician's power came from Satan and not from God. Paul even announced that, as a result of Elymas's deceitful attempt to thwart the purposes of God, the magician would be struck blind for a period of time (vv. 10–11).

The apostles knew that this was no time to be passive or tolerant of Elymas's false beliefs. They responded quickly, demonstrating that the magician's attempts to get in the way of God's work would not be tolerated. In the same way, while we as Christians are called to love and share the Good News of Christ with those who do not know God, we aren't called to blindly accept and endorse their ungodly habits and behaviors. We're commanded to stand up for righteousness! When we speak out in support of the truth, we offer people hope and light instead of silently standing by as they continue to live in sin and darkness.

A Mature Response to Desertion

Next, Paul faced desertion by a close friend and colleague, John Mark. But *when another defected, Paul pressed on.* Paul, Barnabas, and John Mark had sailed from Cyprus to Pamphylia, along the southern coast of what is now Turkey. This land boasted a dangerously rocky, rugged coastline that ascended sharply into a steep mountain range. The sight of these intimidating mountains probably cast fear and doubt into the mind of the young John Mark, who had rarely ventured far from his homeland. Perhaps that fear, paired with homesickness or concern over an illness that Paul contracted, convinced John Mark to jump ship. Without any explanation, Luke wrote simply, "John left them and returned to Jerusalem" (v. 13b).

Despite the hurt and disappointment that Paul and Barnabas must have felt when John Mark left their missionary team, they were undeterred from their mission. They kept their eyes on the goal. They felt abandoned, yet they knew that they still had a job to do. So, keeping their emotions in check, they pressed on.

What an important lesson for us to learn as well! Throughout our lives, throughout our ministries, people will leave. Some will agree with us; some won't. Some may be upset about one aspect or another of our lives or our ministry; some will simply move on. But we must remember that ultimately, we are not called to be people-pleasers. We're called to be God-pleasers! One mark of our maturity as believers is the ability to press on, regardless of who chooses to walk off the scene.

A Mature Response to Unexpected Opportunities

Like Paul, we never know what new and unexpected opportunities God will bring our way when we keep our focus on our mission. *Yet when Paul was invited to speak, he did.* Paul and Barnabas finally arrived in Pisidian Antioch, and when the Sabbath day came, they made their way to the synagogue to worship:

> After the reading of the Law and the Prophets the synagogue officials sent to them, saying, "Brethren, if you have any word of exhortation for the people, say it." Paul stood up, and motioning with his hand said, "Men of Israel, and you who fear God, listen . . ." (vv. 15–16)

Without hesitation, Paul took his cue. He carefully traced the thread of the Gospel through the Old Testament and into the present day. He taught the people what they needed to know regarding the Law, God's view of sin, and God's standard of holiness. Then Paul shared with them how God sent His only Son, Jesus Christ, to fulfill the Old Testament Scriptures and to offer people grace, forgiveness, and freedom from sin.

Impressive! Paul didn't even know that he was going to preach that day, but he was prepared. He demonstrated his ability to "preach the word; be ready in season and out of season; reprove, rebuke, exhort, with great patience and instruction" (2 Tim. 4:2). He recognized how hungry the people were for the Word of God, so he offered them exactly what they needed. Their response was overwhelmingly positive—until the hostile Jewish leaders caught wind of Paul's doings.

A Mature Response to Open Rejection

Even the Gentiles received Paul's message and rejoiced (Acts 13:48), but the Jews bristled. They lashed out at Paul and contradicted his teaching. But *even when Paul was rejected, he didn't quit.* He continued to speak the truth, despite Jewish opposition:

> But when the Jews saw the crowds, they were filled with jealousy and began contradicting the things spoken by Paul, and were blaspheming. Paul and Barnabas spoke out boldly and said, "It was necessary that the word of God be spoken to you first; since you repudiate it and judge yourselves unworthy of eternal life, behold, we are turning to the Gentiles." (vv. 45–46)

Paul learned that every ministry has its critics. They are everywhere—even in the church. We might call these people "joy-stealers." They usually have a negative attitude and a negative response to any given situation. Joy-stealers look for any possible way, any loophole, to oppose the work and the people of God. But when we know our identity, our mission, and our God-given purpose, not even the joy-stealers can stand in our way.

How did Paul and Barnabas persevere through such hostile opposition? They set their sights on things above instead of on temporal things. They didn't depend on the response and accolades of people. Rather, they honored and obeyed God. Fame and recognition weren't their ministry goals.

You'll find that if you focus only on pleasing people, you'll sink like a rock in a country pond! You're doomed to disillusionment if you focus on the temporal. But if you focus on the eternal, God calls you a success. Someday, you will hear Him say, "Well done, good and faithful servant" (Matt. 25:23 NIV)—even if no one on earth ever applauds you.

A Mature Response to Praise

The concept of praise introduces our fifth point regarding Paul's response: *When Paul was inappropriately exalted, he humbly resisted praise.* When Paul and Barnabas "fled to the cities of Lycaonia, Lystra and Derbe" (Acts 14:6), the Lycaonian people worshiped them as gods!

> When the crowds saw what Paul had done, they raised their voice, saying in the Lycaonian language, "The gods have become like men and have come down to us." And they began calling Barnabas, Zeus, and Paul, Hermes, because he was the chief speaker. (vv. 11–12)

But, instead of receiving the people's praise, Paul and Barnabas

> tore their robes and rushed out into the crowd, cry-
> ing out and saying, "Men, why are you doing these
> things? We are also men of the same nature as you,
> and preach the gospel to you that you should turn
> from these vain things to a living God, who made
> the heaven and the earth and the sea and all that
> is in them." (vv. 14–15)

Instead of accepting the people's flattery, Paul and Barnabas were anguished at the Lycaonians' response. The two men resisted this misguided worship, reflecting the praise back to the Lord.

A Mature Response to Unfair Treatment

When Paul was unfairly treated and abused, he persevered. In fact, after being stoned and left for dead in Lystra, he got up and went back into that very city to spend the night (v. 20)! How was the apostle able to endure this abuse? How did he persevere through such horrible circumstances? He refused to set his affection on temporal things. Instead, he trusted God and placed his life in the Lord's hands.

We can learn an important lesson from Paul's perspective: When we focus on the eternal, we can keep going no matter what people say or do. But when we focus on the temporal, we're doomed to disillusionment. The people around Paul praised him as a god one moment and then stoned him the next! Paul learned that he couldn't trust public opinion. This situation also affirmed that fame and fortune aren't the answers to life's problems. King Solomon, the richest and wisest king that ever lived, recognized this truth when he wrote, "Wealth certainly makes itself wings like an eagle that flies toward the heavens" (Prov. 23:5).

Paul succeeded because he sought the praise of God over the praise of men. He persevered and pressed on, no matter how difficult his circumstances. He trusted God for the results of his life's work instead of relying on the opinions of people.

A Mature Response to a Mission Accomplished

When Paul had finished his mission, he must have felt a great sense of accomplishment. Most importantly, *when he returned to places he had been before, he had no regrets.* Though he and Barnabas had encountered numerous obstacles along the way, they had done what they set out to do: proclaim the Gospel throughout Asia Minor. And they had seen God reap a great deal of fruit through their ministry. They were ready to return home and offer an exuberant report of what God had done on their journey.

The Power of an Eternal Perspective

The end of Acts 14 chronicles the return trip of the two men to their home base of Antioch. En route, they visited the cities where they had previously preached the Gospel. They returned to Lystra, where Paul had been stoned and left for dead. They backtracked to Iconium, Pisidian Antioch, then down to Perga and Attalia. Exhausted, yet feeling a sense of accomplishment, they sailed back across the Mediterranean. Their first missionary journey had come to an end.

A second aspect of Paul's journey bears mentioning here. When he returned to tell the people of Antioch about his mission trip, *Paul never forgot that his ministry was about what God had done, not about his own accomplishments.*

> When they had arrived and gathered the church together, they began to report all things that God had done with them and how He had opened a door of faith to the Gentiles. (v. 27)

Paul never forgot that God was the One who gave him the mission and fulfilled it. The work may be ours, but the glory belongs to God. The responsibility is ours to embrace, but the credit belongs to the Lord alone. When we have our focus on the goal, we gain a proper perspective on our lives. We find purpose and fulfillment when we have a firm grasp on our identity, our mission, and our purpose.

Digging Deeper

Are you surprised at how many sorcerers, magicians, and false prophets like Elymas appear in Scripture? Don't be. Satan and his fallen angels have tried to thwart the work of God since the beginning of time. And Christians have always run up against those who attempt to imitate God by counterfeiting His power.

Have you noticed that our culture has become increasingly interested in "pop" occult phenomena? Kids as well as adults experiment with tarot cards and Ouija boards. Many read their horoscopes "just to see what they say." Others watch TV shows such as *Beyond* in which mediums, also called *necromancers*, profess to be able to talk with their clients' deceased relatives. Fascination with other psychic phenomena abounds.

We often tend to think of these activities as harmless. But are they? Let's take a look at what Scripture has to say.

The dictionary defines *necromancy* as "conjuration of the spirits of the dead for purposes of magically revealing the future or influencing the course of events."[2] Probably the best-known biblical example of this is King Saul's clandestine meeting with the witch of Endor in the book of 1 Samuel. God strictly prohibits such activities in Deuteronomy 18:9–14:

> "When you enter the land which the Lord your God gives you, you shall not learn to imitate the detestable things of those nations. There shall not be found among you anyone who makes his son or his daughter pass through the fire, one who uses divination, one who practices witchcraft, or one who interprets omens, or a sorcerer, or one who casts a spell, or a medium, or a spiritist, or one who calls up the dead. For whoever does these things is detestable to the Lord; and because of these detestable things the Lord your God will drive them out before you. You shall be blameless before the Lord your God. For those nations, which you shall dispossess, listen to those who practice witchcraft and to diviners, but as for you, the Lord your God has not allowed you to do so."

Forms of the occult represent Satan and his influences rather than God and His desires. Although some of these activities may seem like harmless fun, think of them as crossover involvements. They may begin as innocent interests or games but could lead to serious entanglement in witchcraft, spiritism, and other occult activities. Using Ouija boards, dealing with psychics, consulting necromancers, or any attempt to contact spirits (demons) can lead to extremely serious consequences.

---

2. *Merriam-Webster's Collegiate Dictionary*, 10th ed., see "necromancy."

What is your background regarding such activities as consulting horoscopes, playing with Ouija boards, contacting psychics, using tarot cards, and so on? Do you have friends who have been involved with these types of activities? According to the Bible, what should your response be to such influences?

_____

_____

_____

_____

_____

_____

How would you describe the way the occult is portrayed in the media?

_____

_____

_____

_____

_____

How can you protect yourself and your family against popular forms and influences of the occult?

_____

_____

_____

_____

Living Insights

Let's address in more detail the three vital elements of a fulfilling life that were covered in this chapter: your sense of personal identity, your sense of mission, and your sense of purpose.

Your Identity

When God looks at you, what do you think He sees? What unique qualities do you possess? How do you define and identify yourself to others?

_____

_____

_____

_____

What spiritual gifts and natural talents has God given you? How are you using these gifts and talents right now? What steps can you take to use these gifts and talents more fully in your marriage, your family, your church, your workplace, and your community?

_____

_____

_____

_____

_____

Your Mission

What do you feel is your personal mission in life?

_____

_____

_____

_____

How do your everyday activities further your mission? What can you do to better carry it out?

_____

_____

_____

_____

Your Purpose

What do you feel are God's purposes for you on earth? If you're not sure, read Deuteronomy 6:5; Micah 6:8; Matthew 28:19–20; Romans 8:28–30; and 1 John 4:7–11.

_____

_____

_____

_____

_____

_____

_____

How well are you living up to these purposes? What changes do you need to make in your life to better reflect them?

_____

_____

_____

_____

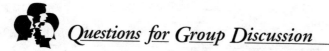 *Questions for Group Discussion*

1. Have you ever been in a situation in which you needed to "step up to the plate" and defend your faith? If so, what were the circumstances? What was your response? What happened as a result of your action or inaction?

2. Have you ever been involved with a project or relationship when someone defected as John Mark did? If so, what happened? How did that make you feel?

3. Have you ever had to speak or perform with little or no previous notice? If so, share your experience with the group. Did you rely on God for help or did you go it alone? What was the result?

4. Have you ever faced persecution or rejection as a result of your relationship with Christ? If so, what happened? What truths from this chapter might apply to that situation?

Chapter 12

THE DAY TWO MISSIONARIES DUKED IT OUT

Acts 15:36–41

Sometimes we hear things that seem completely unbelievable.

Several years ago, a newspaper assigned one of its budding young news reporters to interview Mother Teresa about her sacrificial life-long ministry in the streets of Calcutta, India. The reporter's job was to provide a unique snapshot of this saintly woman's life's work. At one point during the interview, the young man asked Mother Teresa if she had ever dreamed of being anything else. Without a moment's hesitation, she replied, "Well, I always wanted to be a flight attendant!" Can you imagine Mother Teresa in a uniform, serving Cokes and coffee and handing out prepackaged meals on an airplane? Outrageous! But that had once been her dream.[1]

Sometimes our presuppositions don't match reality. Without warning, we encounter a situation so surprising that we're forced to rethink the things we once assumed to be true. The same would happen if we saw two missionaries duking it out over a disagreement. Missionaries? You can't be serious. All missionaries do is pray, share the Gospel, and live sacrificially in foreign countries. Right?

Wrong. Even missionaries have disagreements, as we'll soon find from Luke's surprisingly up-close-and-personal account of a spat between Paul and Barnabas.

A Surprising Disagreement

Nowhere else in Scripture do we encounter a powerhouse ministry team like Paul and Barnabas. But these two passionate pastors were about to lock horns in a difficult conflict.

> After some days Paul said to Barnabas, "Let us return and visit the brethren in every city in which we proclaimed the word of the Lord, and see how

---

1. Charles R. Swindoll, *Paul: A Man of Grace and Grit* (Nashville, Tenn.: The W Publishing Group, 2002), pp. 167–168.

they are." Barnabas wanted to take John, called Mark, along with them also. But Paul kept insisting that they should not take him along who had deserted them in Pamphylia and had not gone with them to the work. (Acts 15:36–38)

Who would ever expect a disagreement between these two men? Their debate began with a positive and visionary idea: Paul's suggestion that they return to the places they had visited on their first missionary journey. Both of them agreed that this visit would benefit all involved. But Barnabas wanted to take John Mark, and Paul didn't.

Paul and Barnabas had opposing perspectives on the same issue. They discussed their viewpoints. They presented their arguments. But they weren't able to come to a compromise or a resolution. Ultimately, they decided to permanently part company:

And there occurred such a sharp disagreement that they separated from one another, and Barnabas took Mark with him and sailed away to Cyprus. But Paul chose Silas and left, being committed by the brethren to the grace of the Lord. And he was traveling through Syria and Cilicia, strengthening the churches. (vv. 39–41)

The situation could have ended tragically, but it didn't. Why? Because Paul and Barnabas agreed to disagree instead of letting their differences destroy their relationship. As far as we know, these two men never crossed paths again. But by parting ways they were able to multiply their efforts in spreading the Gospel. You might call this "multiplying through division"! Instead of allowing their difference of opinion to hinder the Lord's work, they used the disagreement to further it. They created two new ministry teams and set out in opposite directions to share the Gospel.

We wonder what might have occurred if Paul and Barnabas had been able to work through their disagreement and reach a compromise. Surely they would have continued their powerful, life-changing ministry as a team. Perhaps they should have stuck it out, each sacrificing his own desires for the sake of sharing the Gospel. But even though they never worked together again, at least they supported each other and remained friends. From their experience, we can gain a fresh perspective on our own disagreements.

A Fresh Perspective on Disagreements

The ability of Paul and Barnabas to deal with their disagreement offers us some principles to follow when we face conflicts in our own lives. First, recognize that *a disagreement involves one issue but several viewpoints*. Every dispute contains the same two ingredients: an issue, which is objective, and various viewpoints and opinions, which are subjective. Issues involve facts. Viewpoints involve feelings and personalities. Putting these two elements together, we could define a *disagreement* as "a conflict that occurs over an issue seen from opposing points of view." If we can keep these two factors in mind, we'll be better able to stay under control during disagreements.

Second, we must understand that *in a disagreement, each side has validity*. Both sides have strengths, and both sides have weaknesses. Neither side is a slam dunk. The issue in Paul and Barnabas's case posed itself as this question: Should a person who walks away from a serious responsibility be given a second chance? Or, in other words, should someone who leaves people in the lurch be allowed to go on a similar mission again where exactly the same thing might happen? Barnabas said, "Yes! Absolutely. By all means." But Paul said, "No! Absolutely not. By no means." Obviously, each man had his reasons for his viewpoint, and these reasons were supported by both facts and strong emotions.

Barnabas took this point of view: "Yes, John Mark left, but he was inexperienced. We didn't warn him beforehand about the dangers of the trip, and he was afraid and homesick. But we made it, didn't we? And he definitely learned his lesson. He needs encouragement and affirmation right now. We're taking him, and that's final!" Plus, John Mark was Barnabas's cousin. So you can imagine that family ties probably played a role in Barnabas's decision.

Paul, on the other hand, felt the opposite way: "I understand that you want to give John Mark a second chance, but he's not dependable. He's unfaithful. He already deserted us once! This is a vital mission, and there's no room for quitters. Why give him the opportunity to desert us again? We're not taking him, and that's final."

Most of us probably tend to side with Barnabas, thinking, "Oh, why not just go ahead and take him along, Paul? The kid deserves a second chance." But before we make such a quick judgment, let's bring the disagreement into modern times and modern terms.

Would you loan money to a person who had previously borrowed money from you and never paid it back? Would you trust a close friend again who had turned her back on you when you needed her most? Would you loan your car to someone who had wrecked it the last time they borrowed it?

It's funny how our perspective changes when we bring a problem into the present, isn't it? Now we can better understand the tension between Paul and Barnabas. This kind of tension often leads to hurt feelings, which brings us to our last point: *In heated disagreements, someone usually gets hurt.* Often both parties experience anger and hurt feelings. And the greater the heat, the greater the hurt! In order to minimize the negative repercussions of our disagreements, let's examine four positive principles for dealing with conflict.

Four Principles for Dealing with Conflict

From the experience of Paul and Barnabas, we can glean four principles for conflict management. First, *when in disagreement, work hard at seeing both viewpoints—not just your own.* Of course, this can be hard to do. Memorize Philippians 2:3–4 and use it as a reminder whenever you face a conflict:

> Do nothing from selfishness or empty conceit, but with humility of mind regard one another as more important than yourselves; do not merely look out for your own personal interests, but also for the interests of others.

Second, *when both sides have good support, seek a wise compromise.* Neither Paul nor Barnabas was willing to budge on the issue of taking John Mark with them on the journey. Acts 15:39–40 indicates a *sharp* disagreement and then complete separation. This was no small conflict! Perhaps the two men could have come up with some win-win options instead of having to part company; perhaps later in life they even looked back on this decision with regret. Though God blessed their ministries elsewhere, Paul and Barnabas never again reunited in ministry. Before you take drastic measures, seek compromise. This is the best way to salvage your relationship.

Third, *when the conflict persists, care enough to work it through rather than run away.* When we're confronted with conflict, our "flight mechanisms" signal us to run rather than to stay and calmly talk through the issues at hand. For instance, we might be tempted to slam the phone down after a heated argument or to give the other person the silent treatment. We may wish we could bolt from a relationship when times get tough or quit our job because of an "impossible" boss. We might feel like breaking off a long-time friendship or alienating a family member. It's easier to run than to stay and work it out. But when you care enough to deal with a conflict, it shows. And that care goes a long way toward restoring relationships.

Fourth, *when an issue cannot be resolved, graciously agree to disagree*. Don't let conflicts drive a wedge between you and your loved ones. If an issue isn't absolutely essential to your relationship and no resolution or compromise can be reached, drop the matter and try your best not to bring it up again.

When you're upset about a conflict or disagreement, remember the time you have spent investing in your close relationships. As much as possible, try to keep an eternal perspective. It's amazing how someone's heart can change when you show love even in the face of adversity. Remember Philip Melanchthon's wise counsel: "In essentials *unity*. In non-essentials *liberty*. In all things *charity*."[2]

Living Insights

We serve a God of second chances. The Bible contains story after story depicting God's tender mercy and forgiveness toward those who have wronged Him. Throughout Scripture, Jesus continued to love those who turned their backs on Him, denied Him, and even betrayed Him to the death. He sacrificed His life on the cross and rose again in victory over sin and death so that we could gain abundant, eternal life.

Has God given you a second chance? If so, in what way(s)?

_____

_____

_____

_____

_____

2. Philip Melanchthon, as quoted by Charles R. Swindoll in *Paul: A Man of Grace and Grit* (Nashville, Tenn.: The W Publishing Group, 2002), p. 179.

How have others given you a second chance when you needed it?

_____

_____

_____

_____

Is there anyone in your life who didn't give you a second chance when you would have liked one? If so, what were the circumstances? What happened to your relationship with this person as a result?

_____

_____

_____

_____

Now think about your current relationships with others. Are you in a relationship or situation right now in which you need to give someone a second chance? If so, who is it, and what is the situation?

_____

_____

_____

_____

In what specific way can you offer this person a second chance and restore your relationship with him or her?

_____

_____

_____

_____

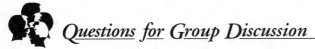

Questions for Group Discussion

1. If you were in the same situation as Paul and Barnabas, would you have given John Mark another chance? Why or why not?

2. Talk about a time when you had a disagreement with someone close to you. What were the circumstances? What happened as a result? Was your relationship with the person strengthened or strained?

3. Do you tend to deal with interpersonal conflicts directly, or do you tend to avoid conflict at all costs? Why do you think you react this way to difficult situations?

4. Are you currently in a situation of conflict with someone? If so, how can you use the four principles of conflict resolution discussed in this chapter to help solve the problem and restore your relationship?

Chapter 13

TRAVELING
AS PAUL TRAVELED
Acts 15:40–16:40

Y ou learn a lot about people when you travel with them! You
observe how they handle unexpected setbacks or changes in
plans. You see how they act when they're hungry, frustrated, or
exhausted from traveling. And many times, you experience a rude
awakening as you discover their true colors!

In contrast, we've discovered that, despite the hardships he faced
along the way, Paul traveled well—not in luxury, but in obedience.
British pastor and author F. B. Meyer wrote:

> If in an unknown country, I am informed that I must
> pass through a valley where the sun is hidden, or
> over a stony bit of road, to reach my abiding place—
> when I come to it, each moment of shadow or jolt
> of the carriage tells me that I am on the right road.[1]

What a fitting summary of Paul's journeys, as well! When God
called Paul, He informed the apostle that he would suffer great
hardship and persecution for the sake of spreading the Gospel. Paul's
trials simply affirmed that he was on the right course! Because he
persevered despite great personal cost, Paul reaped an abundant
harvest for the kingdom of God. Now, let's follow some of Paul's
footsteps on his second missionary journey to understand how he
traveled so well.

A Traveling Team

We'll begin in Antioch, where Paul spent some time resting
and recovering after his first missionary journey. He most likely
experienced extreme fatigue as well as other physical ailments as a
result of his difficulties on the road. No doubt, he was also emotionally shaken after being separated from his longtime friend and
colaborer, Barnabas. Barnabas and his new ministry partner, John

---

1. F. B. Meyer, *Christ in Isaiah*, as quoted by Charles R. Swindoll in *Paul: A Man of Grace
and Grit* (Nashville, Tenn.: The W Publishing Group, 2002), p. 181.

Mark, were already on their way to Cyprus. Paul needed a new traveling companion, so he chose a man named Silas whom the church at Jerusalem had already commissioned for ministry. A seasoned disciple and a Roman citizen, Silas would make a worthy traveling companion for Paul.

Paul Selects Silas

Paul and Silas gathered a few personal belongings and set off on the well-worn path leading from Antioch toward Paul's hometown of Tarsus. As Paul traveled, he undoubtedly felt pangs of homesickness as he smelled the familiar scent of springtime blossoms and saw the gleaming snow-capped peaks of the Taurus Mountains looming in the distance. But Paul and Silas pressed on, heading northward on the road that traversed the rugged, rocky terrain.

> But Paul chose Silas and left, being committed by the brethren to the grace of the Lord. And he was traveling through Syria and Cilicia, strengthening the churches. (Acts 15:40–41)

Together, Paul and Silas set out to deliver the mandate of the Jerusalem Council,[2] taking the Word of God to the Gentiles. As they made their rounds, they made sure that new believers received the instruction, encouragement, and pastoral care they needed. The two men moved northwest to the city of Lystra, where Paul introduced his new companion to a thriving community of Christians.

Paul Taps Timothy

In this group of believers, Paul and Silas met Timothy. Paul immediately recognized this ministry-minded young man as the perfect teammate for their journey. He knew that Timothy's presence would provide an additional measure of friendship, companionship, and accountability.

> Paul came also to Derbe and to Lystra. And a disciple was there, named Timothy, the son of a Jewish woman who was a believer, but his father was a

---

2. Acts 15:1–29 describes a meeting held by the Jerusalem Council in which the apostles discussed whether or not Gentile converts had to be circumcised. James's clear verdict in verse 19 was that Gentile converts need not be circumcised. *The Ryrie Study Bible* (Chicago, Ill.: Moody Press, 1995), pp. 1756–58.

Greek, and he was well spoken of by the brethren who were in Lystra and Iconium. Paul wanted this man to go with him; and he took him and circumcised him because of the Jews who were in those parts, for they all knew that his father was a Greek.[3] (16:1–3)

Once this rite had taken place, Paul, Silas, and Timothy hit the road again to continue carrying out the Lord's work.

Now while they were passing through the cities, they were delivering the decrees which had been decided upon by the apostles and elders who were in Jerusalem, for them to observe. So the churches were being strengthened in the faith, and were increasing in number daily. (vv. 4–5)

Road Closed—Detour!

As these three men ministered, the Holy Spirit guided them toward certain areas and away from others:

They passed through the Phrygian and Galatian region, *having been forbidden by the Holy Spirit to speak the word in Asia;* and after they came to Mysia, they were trying to go into Bithynia, and *the Spirit of Jesus did not permit them;* and passing by Mysia, they came down to Troas. (vv. 6–8, emphasis added)

What? God blocked the path of the Gospel? That's right. The Holy Spirit forbade the men to share the Gospel in Asia, and He also prevented them from going into Bithynia. We see why in the next verses of Acts 16:

A vision appeared to Paul in the night: a man of Macedonia was standing and appealing to him, and saying, "Come over to Macedonia and help us." When he had seen the vision, immediately we

---

3. The Jerusalem Council had declared that circumcision was not necessary for salvation or acceptance into the body of Christ. However, because of Timothy's part-Jewish and part-Gentile background, Paul felt his circumcision would enable Timothy to be a more effective witness. In the case of the Gentile minister Titus, Paul insisted that he not be circumcised (see Gal. 2:3). *The Ryrie Study Bible* (Chicago, Ill.: Moody Press, 1995), p. 1759.

sought to go into Macedonia, concluding that God had called us to preach the gospel to them.

So putting out to sea from Troas, we ran a straight course to Samothrace, and on the day following to Neapolis; and from there to Philippi, which is a leading city of the district of Macedonia, a Roman colony; and we were staying in this city for some days. (vv. 9–12)

Notice that the gospel writer Luke began using the pronoun "we" in verse 10. He joined Paul, Silas, and Timothy on their journey as they set sail for Macedonia.

A remarkable encounter would soon take place between these four men and some women who had gathered along their new route. God had set up a divine appointment.

A Better Way

And on the Sabbath day we went outside the gate to a riverside, where we were supposing that there would be a place of prayer; and we sat down and began speaking to the women who had assembled. A woman named Lydia, from the city of Thyatira, a seller of purple fabrics, a worshiper of God, was listening; and the Lord opened her heart to respond to the things spoken by Paul. And when she and her household had been baptized, she urged us, saying, "If you have judged me to be faithful to the Lord, come into my house and stay." And she prevailed upon us. (vv. 13–15)

Now we see why God closed the door to Asia and Bithynia! He wanted these faithful men to share the Good News with a group of women who sought to know Him. As a result, a window was opened—the window of Lydia's heart. She rejoiced over the Gospel message, and she and her household chose to be baptized as an expression of their new relationship with Christ.

A Perilous Passage

Paul and his companions soon experienced a divine encounter of a different sort with another woman—a slave-girl with the ability to tell fortunes.

> It happened that as we were going to the place of prayer, a slave-girl having a spirit of divination met us, who was bringing her masters much profit by fortune-telling. . . . [Paul] turned and said to the spirit, "I command you in the name of Jesus Christ to come out of her!" And it came out at that very moment. (vv. 16–18)

You'd think the townspeople would have rejoiced at this slave-girl's release from the demon's cruel torment. But instead, they grabbed Paul and Silas and dragged them before the religious authorities. The chief magistrates and the members of the crowd reacted, fiercely attacking these men who had interrupted their way of life:

> The crowd rose up together against them, and the chief magistrates tore their robes off them and proceeded to order them to be beaten with rods. When they had struck them with many blows, they threw them into prison, commanding the jailer to guard them securely; and he, having received such a command, threw them into the inner prison and fastened their feet in the stocks. (vv. 22–24)

Stripped. Beaten with rods. Thrown into prison. These men must have wondered, "But Lord, weren't we doing what You called us to do? Didn't we go where You wanted us to go?" Yes, they did. And this was part of their call. This was one of the harsh requirements of their ministry.

Remember that when you face turmoil, difficulty, persecution, and hardship, you aren't necessarily out of God's will. You might be smack-dab in the middle of it! When you face obstacles along your journey, recognize that God always has a reason and a plan to redeem your trials. This would soon be evident in the case of Paul and Silas.

Travel Tunes

Paul and Silas sat in a filthy jail cell, bruised and battered, with their flesh torn to shreds by the soldiers' rods. Instead of nursing their wounds and crying out to God about the unfairness of it all, however, these two men did the most amazing thing—they worshiped God:

> But about midnight Paul and Silas were praying and singing hymns of praise to God, and the prisoners were listening to them; and suddenly there came a

great earthquake, so that the foundations of the prison house were shaken; and immediately all the doors were opened and everyone's chains were unfastened. (vv. 25–26)

Another incredible miracle! We've seen God work in some amazing ways throughout Paul's journeys. Here, God heard the praises of His faithful men and sent an earthquake to shake the prison foundations and loose the chains that bound the prisoners. When the terrified jailer realized what had happened, he assumed the prisoners had made a mad dash for the door. He prepared to take his own life rather than be killed by the Romans for allowing the prisoners to escape (v. 27).

But Paul cried out with a loud voice, saying, "Do not harm yourself, for we are all here!" And he called for lights and rushed in, and trembling with fear he fell down before Paul and Silas, and after he brought them out, he said, "Sirs, what must I do to be saved?" They said, "Believe in the Lord Jesus, and you will be saved, you and your household." And they spoke the word of the Lord to him together with all who were in his house. (vv. 28–32)

Like a sword, the Holy Spirit pierced the jailer's heart to the core. Paul and Silas shared the message of the Gospel with this man and his entire family. Rejoicing, they believed the message and professed faith in God. The jailer then rushed to show kindness to the two men who had ministered to him:

And he took them that very hour of the night and washed their wounds, and immediately he was baptized, he and all his household. And he brought them into his house and set food before them, and rejoiced greatly, having believed in God with his whole household. (vv. 33–34)

Freedom Trail

The next day, the chief magistrates sent their policemen to release Paul and Silas. But Paul said to them:

"They have beaten us in public without trial, men who are Romans, and have thrown us into prison; and now are they sending us away secretly? No indeed! But let them come themselves and bring us out." (v. 37)

When the chief magistrates heard that the two men were Romans, their knees began to knock! They had illegally beaten and jailed the men without giving them a proper trial. So they quickly changed their tune. The magistrates rushed to meet Paul and Silas, escorted them from prison, and begged them to leave the city.

The freed missionaries immediately went to encourage Lydia and some other believers at her home. After they had finished their ministry there, our faithful friends set out for the city of Thessalonica for the next step of their adventure (v. 40).

Four Principles for Traveling Well

From Paul's experiences on the road, we can glean four principles that will guide us on our own journeys.

First of all, *when you travel, don't go alone.* Find at least one companion to accompany you on your journey. Ideally, this would be your spouse, a close family member, or a trusted friend. Remember all the traveling companions Paul had over the years? Barnabas. John Mark. Silas. Timothy. Luke. Aquila and Priscilla. And don't forget Sopater, Aristarchus, Secundus, Gaius, Timothy, Tychicus, Trophimus, and Erastus! We don't spend much time thinking about these people, yet Paul considered them indispensable to his ministry. They encouraged and enabled him.

Remember to choose your companions wisely. If you become lonely, they will be there to keep you company. If you feel sad, they can encourage you and help lift your spirits. If something goes wrong, your partners will be there to assist you. Remember that Ecclesiastes 4:9–12 says two are better than one! And three are better than two!

Second, *when you travel, don't lose touch with friends and family.* When Paul traveled, he stayed accountable. His heart stayed close to home. He kept in touch. He wrote letters, provided reports, and gave account of his ministry. He may have kept a journal as well. Although we can't be sure of that, journaling is an excellent means of leaving a lasting legacy of your spiritual journey to your loved ones. It's not a record of what you've done hour by hour or day by day; that's a diary. In a journal, you record thoughts, feelings, experiences, and milestones in your spiritual journey. You share the lessons you have learned in your walk with the Father. If you don't already keep a journal, consider it! How meaningful this can be to those who follow in your footsteps!

Paul's epistles could be considered inspired journal entries. He recorded milestones along the way so that believers could follow in his footsteps and learn the same lessons that he learned. In this way, the apostle left a lasting legacy for his children and grandchildren in the faith.

Third, *when you travel, don't believe everything you hear!* Use your head and avoid passing judgment on people or situations until you have enough information. Often, on life's journey, you'll encounter one of two situations: either people will place you on a pedestal and treat you like royalty, or they'll look down their noses at you and treat you like a pauper. Paul found that he was worshiped one moment and despised the next! But he neither let the adulation go to his head, nor did he allow the brutal treatment to dissuade him from the mission God had given him. He refused to take his eyes off his goal.

Some of God's greatest instruments of change have been mistreated, misunderstood, and maligned. Just think about all that Jesus went through, and He was sinless! God uses trials to prepare His servants for the work He has called them to do. God controls every circumstance and uses every situation to further His perfect plan. So focus on obediently following God and graciously interacting with all those you meet on your journey. And take everything you hear with a grain of salt!

Finally, *when you travel, don't become aloof.* It's easy to become distant, untouchable, and superficial when you travel, especially when you're being greatly used of God. Staying real takes commitment. Listening requires effort. Remaining available demands personal sacrifice. Building solid relationships means reaching out to others, even though you might be more comfortable staying in your shell. Remember that people want the *real* you, not a *perfect* you.

Paul seized every opportunity to build relationships while he traveled. He asked Timothy to join him. He sang with Silas while locked in a dark, miserable prison cell. He welcomed Luke as a partner in ministry. He defended his friends. He poured out his heart. He listened. He preached. He laughed. He cried. In the same way, we're called to reach out to those we meet on our life's journey. Just being in the right place at the right time and speaking the right word can touch a person's heart in a way that he or she will never forget. Keep in mind the lessons you've learned from Paul's journey, and you're guaranteed to travel well—not in luxury, but in obedience.

Ever heard the saying, "When God closes a door, He always opens a window"? It's certainly true. Let's take some time to reflect on how God shuts doors and opens windows in our own lives.

When have you experienced a "closed door" in your life? How did you feel during this time?

_____

_____

_____

_____

How did this closed door affect your attitude, your relationships, and your spiritual walk?

_____

_____

_____

_____

Once this period was over, could you see the hand of God in the situation? Why do you think the Lord closed the door on this opportunity?

_____

_____

_____

_____

Do you feel that God eventually opened a window for you regarding this situation? If so, in what ways?

_____

_____

_____

 *Questions for Group Discussion*

1. Who are your favorite travel companions? Why?

2. Have you ever taken a trip alone? If so, how did this trip differ from those you have taken with family or friends?

3. How has God used your experiences on the road to help you grow and mature in your spiritual walk?

4. How have your travel experiences affected your relationships with others?

Chapter 14

PREACHING AS PAUL PREACHED

Acts 17:15–34

Back in the sixteenth century, as the great Italian painter Raphael was painstakingly adding the finishing touches to one of his Vatican frescoes, two rather arrogant cardinals approached. The two began to criticize the artist's masterpiece. One of them rudely announced, "The face of the apostle Paul is much too red." With hardly a glance at the two cardinals, Raphael replied, "He blushes to see into whose hands the church has fallen." [1]

The artist's comment still holds true. The apostle Paul might blush if he saw the state of some of our churches today. The tireless servant and impassioned preacher would no doubt remind us of our responsibility to preach and teach the Word of God. He'd exhort us to share the joy of our salvation and the Good News of our faith with everyone we meet. He might also remind us that if we're Christians, we're in the ministry! Whether we're a senior pastor, lay leader, musician, music minister, nursery worker, counselor, or anyone else in the body of Christ, we're charged with the Great Commission—to take God's truth to an unbelieving world.

When it comes to preaching and teaching God's Word, too many churches provide entertaining sermonettes instead of real sermons. They offer hors d'oeuvres instead of a balanced, nutritious meal. This means that many of us end up eating spiritual junk food instead of taking in the nourishing meat of the Word. Instead of sitting down to a leisurely, lavish feast with all the trimmings, we end up scarfing down a Happy Meal. As a result, we're left unsatisfied and longing for more.

Paul addressed this problem in his second letter to Timothy. In *The Message*, Eugene Peterson paraphrased Paul's comments this way:

> You're going to find that there will be times when
> people will have no stomach for solid teaching, but
> will fill up on spiritual junk food—catchy opinions

---

1. Raphael Sanzio, as quoted by Charles R. Swindoll in *Paul: A Man of Grace and Grit* (Nashville, Tenn.: The W Publishing Group, 2002), p. 200.

that tickle their fancy. They'll turn their backs on truth and chase mirages. But you—keep your eye on what you're doing; accept the hard times along with the good; keep the Message alive; do a thorough job as God's servant. (2 Tim. 4:3–5 THE MESSAGE)[2]

Paul exhorted Timothy to give people what they *needed* to hear, not just what they *wanted* to hear. And the apostle modeled this in his own life, as well. In contrast with those who offer spiritual junk food from the pulpit, Paul offered real spiritual sustenance. Let's examine his ministry in the city of Athens to see how he effectively shared the Word with others.

Entering the Scene

In Acts 17:15, the gospel writer Luke noted that Paul reached the city of Athens alone. While Paul awaited the return of his ministry partners, Silas and Timothy, he walked from the outskirts of the city toward the bustling metropolis.

Paul had received a top-notch religious and cultural education, so he surely looked forward to this encounter with the luxury, beauty, and sophistication of the Greek culture. Ancient Athens boasted exquisite sculpture and architecture, a sixty-thousand-seat stadium, and many art galleries. Lavishly decorated music halls and respected academies of higher learning lined the magnificent stone-paved streets.

In many ways, Athens stood as the cultural center of the entire Greek world. It also represented a philosopher's dream. Great teachers like Socrates, Plato, Aristotle, and Epicurus made their homes there. The loftiest philosophy came from the direction of the Areopagus, also called Mars Hill, which still stands today. Philosophers, teachers, scholars, and historians gathered there to discuss and debate their opinions with others. To them, truth was relative. They knew no absolutes.

Then Paul came into the picture, bringing the Gospel with him.

Recognizing the Need

As the apostle entered Athens, his spirit recoiled in horror. Instead of the lovely cultural metropolis he had expected, Paul found

2. Eugene Peterson, *The Message* (Colorado Springs, Colo.: NavPress, 2002), p. 2172.

a spiritually oppressed, pagan city littered with thousands of idols. He saw people worshiping in shrines, burning incense, weeping, cutting themselves with stones, and offering sacrifices to strange gods. As he roamed through the streets, the apostle passed numerous altars built of stone, wood, and precious metals.

Darkness and spiritual oppression hung over Athens like an ominous cloud. Paul's heart grew heavy and his spirit churned within him as he grew more and more aware of the evil pervading the city:

> Now while Paul was waiting for them at Athens, his spirit was being provoked within him as he was observing the city full of idols. (v. 16)

Paul knew that God, through the Holy Spirit, was calling him to minister to these misled idol-worshipers. So the apostle set out to shine light into their darkness by sharing the hope of Christ with them. Paul modeled four principles of effective communication that we can also use to reach those around us with the Gospel.

Four Principles for Effectively Communicating Biblical Truth

First, *always stay on the subject—Christ*. This remains the most important commandment of communicating the Word of God. Paul kept Christ as his focus as he discussed philosophy and theology with the people of Athens:

> So he was reasoning in the synagogue with the Jews and the God-fearing Gentiles, and in the market place every day with those who happened to be present. And also some of the Epicurean and Stoic philosophers were conversing with him. Some were saying, "What would this idle babbler wish to say?" Others, "He seems to be a proclaimer of strange deities,"—because he was preaching Jesus and the resurrection. (vv. 17–18)

As Paul asked questions and debated issues with his audience, he always kept his final goal in mind, which was to turn people toward Jesus. The apostle knew that preaching and teaching that don't exalt Christ are empty, devoid of meaning and power. Paul wrote to the Corinthian believers, "For I determined to know nothing among you except Jesus Christ, and Him crucified" (1 Cor. 2:2). Paul knew that when Christ's love is preached, lives are radically transformed.

Second, *always speak the truth without fear*. Paul spoke to the Athenians with boldness and wisdom. He waited to disclose the way to the true God until he had the information necessary to be able to effectively share the Gospel with the Athenian people. He also earned the people's trust by waiting for an invitation before he began to speak. And he finally got the invitation he had hoped for!

> And they took him and brought him to the Areopagus, saying, "May we know what this new teaching is which you are proclaiming? For you are bringing some strange things to our ears; so we want to know what these things mean." (Now all the Athenians and the strangers visiting there used to spend their time in nothing other than telling or hearing something new.) (Acts 17:19–21)

The people of Athens accompanied Paul to Mars Hill and asked him to share his message with them. Paul wasted no time in fearlessly communicating the Good News of Christ to his audience:

> So Paul stood in the midst of the Areopagus and said, "Men of Athens, I observe that you are very religious in all respects. For while I was passing through and examining the objects of your worship, I also found an altar with this inscription, 'TO AN UNKNOWN GOD.' Therefore what you worship in ignorance, this I proclaim to you. The God who made the world and all things in it, since He is Lord of heaven and earth, does not dwell in temples made with hands; nor is He served by human hands, as though He needed anything, since He Himself gives to all people life and breath and all things; and He made from one man every nation of mankind to live on all the face of the earth, having determined their appointed times and the boundaries of their habitation, that they would seek God, if perhaps they might grope for Him and find Him, though He is not far from each one of us; for in Him we live and move and exist, as even some of your own poets have said, 'For we also are His children.'" (vv. 22–28)

When Paul addressed his audience, he hooked them immediately by first complimenting them and then sharing his observations about their values. They were "very religious" people who tried to appease the gods. But they were not Christians. There's a big difference between practicing empty rituals and experiencing a relationship with the living God! Paul made that point extremely clear.

Paul began his speech by saying, "Men of Athens, I observe that you are very religious in all respects. . . . What you worship in ignorance, this I proclaim to you" (vv. 22b, 23b). He started with *what the people knew* and led them to discover *what they did not know.* Paul recognized the people's desire to know and worship a true God, One who loved them, One with power. So Paul showed them the way to faith in God through Christ. Instead of leaving them in ignorance and fear, he offered them hope.

Good communicators sense the needs of individuals and then speak to those needs without fear. They aren't intimidated by status, gender, or pedigree. They simply speak the truth to all who need to hear it and trust the Lord for the results.

Third, *always start where your audience is.* Paul definitely knew how to fish for men! Before he shared the Gospel with the Athenians, he spent time getting to know them. He built bridges to span the gap between himself and the people. He patiently and respectfully asked questions in order to learn about their culture, their traditions, their beliefs, and their religious practices. Only then did he address their spiritual needs. Only then did he reveal that the only Way to the Father is through Jesus Christ, the Son:

> "Being then the children of God, we ought not to think that the Divine Nature is like gold or silver or stone, an image formed by the art and thought of man. Therefore having overlooked the times of ignorance, God is now declaring to men that all people everywhere should repent, because He has fixed a day in which He will judge the world in righteousness through a Man whom He has appointed, having furnished proof to all men by raising Him from the dead." (vv. 29–31)

Usually, it's not difficult for us to accept that we worship an invisible God. But this concept was completely foreign to the people of Athens. A God we can't see? A God who doesn't live in temples made with hands? A God who desires repentance? A God who loves? A God who judges? A God who sacrifices His own Son?

Some were skeptical, but some were intrigued and wanted to hear more. And a few even believed Paul's message:

> Now when they heard of the resurrection of the dead, some began to sneer, but others said, "We shall hear you again concerning this." So Paul went out of their midst. But some men joined him and believed, among whom also were Dionysius the Areopagite and a woman named Damaris and others with them. (vv. 32–34)

Most preachers, teachers, and communicators today encounter the same three types of responses. Some members of the audience may criticize or reject the message for one reason or another. Others are intrigued enough to return for a second hearing. But a precious few have the faith to believe the message and take it to heart.

Fourth, *always surrender the results to God.* We're responsible to help others hear and understand the Gospel message. After that, we must trust God for the results. Remember: we may prepare the patient, but the Lord does the heart surgery!

Paul spoke what he spoke because he felt as he felt. And he felt as he felt because he saw what he saw! He recognized a need, and he acted upon it. He effectively demonstrated that those who communicate the Gospel shouldn't just speak; they also must *listen.* Paul tuned in to the nonverbal as well as the verbal cues of his audience. And as he discerned the gnawing, empty chasm in the souls of those around him, he built a bridge across that chasm using the Cross of Christ.

We aren't called to manipulate others or force them to respond to God's message. Like Paul, we're called to simply follow God's lead and communicate what He desires us to share. When you have the opportunity to reach out, do it. Listen. Care. Pray. Trust God. And try not to keep score. When you trust the Lord for the fruit of your labors, you'll reap a rich harvest of blessings.

Living Insights

Let's take the four principles of communication that we've just discussed and apply them to our own lives, ministries, and relationships.

With whom do you communicate on a regular basis? For example, you might list your spouse, your parents, your children, other family members, friends, clients, coworkers, church members, those in the community, and so on.

_____

_____

_____

_____

Are any of these people non-Christians? If so, commit to sharing your faith and an encouraging word with them. How can you make an effort this week to introduce the subject of Christ to these people?

_____

_____

_____

_____

Paul spoke the truth without fear. What truths do your family members and friends listed above need to hear?

_____

_____

_____

_____

Paul started where his audience was. How can you use the values and experiences you have in common to build bridges to your friends and family members who do not know God?

_____

_____

_____

_____

Paul surrendered the results of his ministry to God. Using the lines below, write a prayer to God. Intercede for your friends, and commit to obeying the Lord's lead and relinquishing the results of your obedience to Him.

_____

_____

_____

_____

_____

Remember to keep praying for divine opportunities to share the Gospel with those you meet on life's journey. When God opens the door for you to reach out to someone, take the initiative to speak the truth in love. Then trust the Lord with the results!

 *Questions for Group Discussion*

1. Are you involved in any ministry or area of service at your church? If so, how might you use that avenue to share Christ's message and His love?

2. Why do you think churches are tempted to offer entertainment rather than preach the Word of God? How have you seen this demonstrated in our culture?

3. Have you ever come in contact with people who worship idols or been to places where false gods were worshiped? If so, how did you feel when faced with this situation?

4. All of us interact with people who need to hear the Gospel. Who are these people in your life? How can you use Paul's four communication principles to reach them?

Chapter 15

LEADING AS PAUL LED

1 Thessalonians 2:1–12

September 11, 2001. In an instant, American confidence crumbled under the rubble of the twin towers. The brutal attack wrenched us out of our comfort zone and thrust our leaders into the combat zone. Early in his presidency, George W. Bush responded to the tragedy with mature moxie. On that terrible Tuesday, Bush mourned with Americans. The next day, he set the country on a course of careful action rather than rash reaction. Bush pulled a knocked-down nation to her feet. Acting with decisive direction, the man we call commander in chief proved worthy of his title.

But true leaders need no title; we follow them out of desire. Positional leaders rely on titles and power; we follow them out of obligation. Before meeting Jesus, Saul of Tarsus—the hungry political leader—prided himself in his position. He used it to wield power over others. After his conversion, Saul—the humbled Christ-follower—boasted in his weakness. Relying on the Lord's strength, he influenced others to follow Christ and began to shepherd new churches with his distinctive leadership style.

Leading with Authenticity

While ministering in Corinth, he wrote to Thessalonica exhorting the believers and defending his apostleship.

> For you yourselves know, brethren, that our coming to you was not in vain, but after we had already suffered and been mistreated in Philippi, as you know, we had the boldness in our God to speak to you the gospel of God amid much opposition. For our exhortation does not come from error or impurity or by way of deceit; but just as we have been approved by God to be entrusted with the gospel, so we speak, not as pleasing men, but God who examines our hearts. For we never came with flattering speech, as you know, nor with a pretext for greed—God is witness—nor did we seek glory from men, either from you or from others, even though

as apostles of Christ we might have asserted our authority. (1 Thess. 2:1–6)

Do you hear the familiarity in Paul's tone? Paul knew the Thessalonians, and they knew him. He was no tent-making mogul with an appointment-juggling assistant, but a coworker who shared their ho-hums and their hallelujahs. Notice the way he reminded his friends of their history together:

For you yourselves know, brethren . . . (v. 1)

After we had already suffered and been mistreated in Philippi, *as you know . . .* (v. 2)

We never came with flattering speech, *as you know . . .* (v. 5)

For you *recall . . .* (v. 9)

You are witnesses . . . (v. 10)

The Thessalonians had seen Paul's suffering. They had marked his mistreatment. Some had cleaned his cuts, bandaged his bruises. Those who bound his broken body felt his pain. They knew he had "been there, done that." He was authentic. And his leadership style showed it.

From Paul's words, we can glean two principles on how to lead with authenticity. First, *Paul did not offer mere theoretical ideals.* No aimless hypothesizing in this classroom! Paul drew his lectures on leadership from his time in the lab. The Thessalonians lived and worked alongside him. They learned the tenets of leadership by watching Paul. As J. Oswald Sanders noted:

We can lead others only as far along the road as we ourselves have traveled. Merely pointing the way is not enough. If we are not walking, then no one can be following, and we are not leading anyone.[1]

Paul wanted the believers at Thessalonica to follow him as he followed Christ. Just as Paul expected the Thessalonians to increase their spiritual strength by following in his spiritual footsteps, we too should grow by pursuing Christ's path.

1. J. Oswald Sanders, *Spiritual Leadership,* 2d ed. (Chicago, Ill.: Moody Press, 1994), p. 28.

Second, *Paul's leadership was neither aloof nor secretive.* John Stott writes,

> Paul's ministry in Thessalonica had been public. It was exercised in the open before God and human beings for he had nothing whatever to hide. Happy are those Christian leaders today, who hate hypocrisy and love integrity, who have nothing to conceal or be ashamed of, who are well known for who and what they are, and who are able to appeal without fear to God and the public as their witnesses![2]

Paul was an open book! In today's terms, they knew his address, his phone number, and his e-mail address. He ate burgers at their cookouts and sold them two tents for the price of one. He never hung the "do not disturb" sign on his door after church.

Paul was approachable and available. An open person has nothing to hide. But if a leader hides behind locked doors and drawn blinds, be wary about following him or her. An unapproachable, inaccessible, invulnerable leader lives inconsistently.

Leading as Paul Led

In reflecting on his time in Thessalonica, Paul reminded the Thessalonians, "You yourselves know, brethren, that our coming to you was not in vain" (1 Thess. 2:1). In effect he was saying, "I consider my time with you well spent"—well spent in fellowship and in suffering. Don't forget that Paul limped into Thessalonica after being beaten in Philippi, but his spirit wasn't battered.

> After we had already suffered and been mistreated in Philippi, as you know, we had the boldness in our God to speak to you the gospel of God amid much opposition. (v. 2)

Paul's secret to success: *He kept on.* No matter his circumstance, he persevered, always stepping closer to the Cross. By illuminating the course to the Cross, Paul blazed the trail for others to follow.

---

2. John R. W. Stott, *The Message of 1 and 2 Thessalonians* from The Bible Speaks Today series, as quoted by Charles R. Swindoll in *Paul: A Man of Grace and Grit* (Nashville, Tenn.: The W Publishing Group, 2002), p. 219.

From Paul's effective leadership example detailed in 1 Thessalonians 2:1–12, we can glean eight principles—four negative, four positive. We are "not to be" the negatives. We are "to be" the positives.

The "Not To Be's"

First, *good leaders are not to be deceptive.*

> For our exhortation does not come from error or impurity or by way of deceit. (v. 3)

Paul did not manipulate his followers through schemes or shams. There were no innuendoes of impurity or dirty dealing in his ministry. He was not a double-talker, but a straight shooter. Not "by way of deceit" means nothing underhanded or devious. Paul never pulled a bait and switch. He explained the rewards of discipleship as well as the price of suffering. He never sugarcoated the costs. Honesty and integrity marked his words.

Today's leaders must strive to cultivate such impervious character. General Dwight D. Eisenhower once wrote,

> To have followers, one must have their confidence. Hence, the supreme quality for a leader is unquestionable integrity. If one's associates find him or her guilty of phoniness, if they find that he lacks forthright integrity, he will fail. His teachings and actions must square with each other.[3]

Second, *good leaders are not to be people-pleasers.*

> . . . but just as we have been approved by God to be entrusted with the gospel, so we speak, not as pleasing men, but God who examines our hearts. (1 Thess. 2:4)

An insistence on being liked by everyone reeks of personal insecurity. People-pleasers value peace at any price. They remain neutral to avoid being alienated. Paul had learned to please not his human audience, but his divine audience of one. He spoke not "as pleasing men, but God who examines our hearts." He chose to tell people what they needed to hear rather than what they wanted to hear. No tickling of his flock's ears.

---

3. Dwight D. Eisenhower, *Quote/Unquote*, as quoted by Charles R. Swindoll in *Paul*, p. 221.

A decisive leader will follow his or her conscience even if it means disappointing the crowd. Leaders need to direct people, not seek the popular vote. A warning: This truth does not justify bull-dozing other believers. Don't throw out tact in the name of truth. A good leader can oppose popular opinion without offending everyone.

Look at the word *flattering* in the next verse.

> For we never came with flattering speech . . .
> (v. 5a)

Paul wanted people's words to reflect their hearts. In order for that to happen, we must focus on "God who examines our hearts" (v. 4). That means we listen closely to Him. If we don't know an answer, we say so. If we do know, we must speak with conviction. Inevitably, some won't like our words. If they leave, we should graciously say goodbye and continue speaking the truth in love.

Third, *good leaders are not to be greedy.*

> . . . nor with a pretext for greed—God is witness.
> (v. 5b)

Godly leaders never use verbal smoke-and-mirror tricks to take advantage of others. The dark side of articulate leaders dwells in their ability to manipulate others. They can easily weave words to get their own way. Too often a discontent heart sows self-serving greed. Greedy leaders hurt their followers as they hoard the glory.

Finally, *good leaders are not to be self-serving.*

> . . . nor did we seek glory from men, either from
> you or from others, even though as apostles of Christ
> we might have asserted our authority. (v. 6)

The apostles and early church leaders were the Lord's cabinet, His crucial men for critical times. Using incredible discernment and wisdom, they exercised their authority with great restraint. They always asserted their power to achieve God's purposes rather than to promote their own agendas.

In *The Reaper*, A. W. Tozer notes:

> "A true and safe leader is likely to be one who has
> no desire to lead, but is forced into a position by the
> inward pressure of the Holy Spirit and the press of
> [circumstances]. . . . There was hardly a great leader
> from Paul to the present day but was drafted by the

Holy Spirit for the task, and commissioned by the Lord to fill a position he had little heart for. . . . The man who is ambitious to lead is disqualified as a leader. The true leader will have no desire to lord it over God's heritage, but will be humble, gentle, self-sacrificing and altogether ready to follow when the Spirit chooses another to lead."[4]

Good leaders don't throw their weight around, don't try to impress others with their importance, don't take unfair advantage. Instead, they serve others. They make no provision for the seeds of deception, people-pleasing, greed, or arrogance. Good leaders root out the negatives and cultivate the positives.

The "To Be's"

First, *good leaders are to be sensitive to others' needs.* Paul continued,

> But we proved to be gentle among you, as a nursing mother tenderly cares for her own children. (1 Thess. 2:7)

Like a nursing mother, Paul was aware of and provided for the needs of others. If you are a leader, cultivate a gentle, nurturing spirit (Gal. 5:23). After the terror of September 11, Mayor Rudolph Giuliani nurtured New Yorkers. He grieved with them at Ground Zero. He wept with those waiting to find loved ones. His tears encouraged citizens to draw strength from their sorrow. His compassion let stoics know that gentleness brings strength. Americans needed to see a gentle leader weep.

Christians must model the same vulnerability. Acting as though we're superhuman does not demonstrate super leadership. Gentleness marked the apostle known for grace and grit.

Second, *good leaders are to be affectionate toward people.*

> Having so fond an affection for you, we were well-pleased to impart to you not only the gospel of God but also our own lives, because you had become very dear to us. (1 Thess. 2:8)

---

4. A. W. Tozer, *The Reaper,* as quoted by J. Oswald Sanders in *Spiritual Leadership,* 2d ed. (Chicago, Ill.: Moody Press, 1994), pp. 29–30.

Paul genuinely enjoyed the people to whom he ministered. What an amazing concept! A minister who likes people. If you don't like people, don't try to lead them. If you crave leadership more than you love your followers, you are not called to serve. You can't lead without love. Love leaves people full when words fall flat.

How do you demonstrate love to those you lead? Try performing small yet frequent acts of kindness and communicating your appreciation to others through spoken encouragement and written words. Take the time to notice people. Leaders who walk over people leave their followers with dusty footprints on their backs. Bossing is easy. Leading is challenging.

Third, *good leaders are to be authentic.*

> You recall, brethren, our labor and hardship. . . . You are witnesses, and so is God, how devoutly and uprightly and blamelessly we behaved toward you believers. (vv. 9–10)

Paul shared the ups and downs of his life with the Thessalonians. His model of transparency, vulnerability, and integrity is one for all of us to follow. The truth he delivered through his lips was the same truth he modeled in his life. The Thessalonians watched the diligence in his work, the thoughtfulness in his actions, the devotion of his calling, and the purity in his life. They knew Paul was the real deal.

Last, *good leaders are to enthusiastically affirm other people.*

> . . . just as you know how we were exhorting and encouraging and imploring each one of you as a father would his own children, so that you would walk in a manner worthy of the God who calls you into His own kingdom and glory. (vv. 11–12)

Paul says we are to cheer people on like a father rooting for his children! Ever sat in front of the star quarterback's father at a Friday night football game? More than likely, his words still echo in your ears.

> Scramble, Frank. Scramble! No, not that way—the other way. Number 23, Frank. He's wide open on the 30. Yes! You nailed it! Straight to him. Beautiful pass! Did you see that?!

You not only saw it. You heard every detail in DSS—Daddy Surround Sound. Was his commentary irritating? Yes. Was his encouragement contagious? For sure.

Just as our kids need compassionate coaching, God's children long for loving leadership. Good leadership balances an affirming father's exhortation with a nursing mother's tenderness. Encouragement waters a parched soul. A good leader pours out the pitcher of refreshment on his people.

Paul valued enthusiastic affirmation. His encouragement inspired people to follow him, and he led them to the Cross. He desired God's people to "walk in a manner worthy of the God who calls you into His own kingdom and glory" (v. 12). That's it. We lead like this so that others will live like that. And it all starts with Christ.

Living Insights

Will you emulate Paul's leadership style if God grants you the responsibility of shepherding others?

On your road with the Lord, are you walking in such a way that you would want a younger believer following your footsteps? If not, what needs to change? If so, are you intentionally influencing someone who needs to mature in his or her walk?

_____

_____

_____

Does your inner person match the face you present to the world? Name three areas in your life in which you need to improve your authenticity.

_____

_____

_____

Paul led with authenticity because he followed the Master's lead. Philippians 2:5–8 shows us that Jesus led with humility:

> Have this attitude in yourselves which was also in Christ Jesus, who, although He existed in the form of God, did not regard equality with God a thing to be grasped, but emptied Himself, taking the form of

a bond-servant, and being made in the likeness of men. Being found in appearance as a man, He humbled Himself by becoming obedient to the point of death, even death on a cross.

How did Christ model servant leadership?

_____

_____

_____

_____

_____

_____

How does Christ's leadership model differ from the world's leadership style?

_____

_____

_____

_____

_____

If God called His Son, who had no proud motives, to humble Himself for our sakes, what does this say about our need to lead by serving?

_____

_____

_____

_____

_____

Questions for Group Discussion

In order to lead effectively, we must be intentional about cultivating our spiritual growth. Those we influence will plant the same seeds we do. If we sow productive seeds in our lives, those who look to us for guidance will reap spiritual benefits in their lives. If we fail to uproot our sinful weeds, those very weeds will choke our disciples' growth too.

1. Good leaders make no provision for the seeds of deception, people-pleasing, greed, or arrogance. Which of these four "weeds" is rooted most deeply in your life? Talk with the group about ways you might uproot it.

2. What verses in the Bible address the uprooting of that weed? Determine to uproot it by making one of these verses your motto.

3. Good leaders sense others' needs, express affection for their people, pursue authenticity, and affirm their flocks. Which of these four qualities need to grow in your life?

4. What verses address fertilizing these qualities in your life? Make these Scriptures food for thought.

Chapter 16

RESPONDING
AS PAUL RESPONDED
Selected Scriptures

Today, a tree at Jerusalem's Holocaust Museum flourishes safely behind a chain link fence. The tree honors Corrie ten Boom's sacrifice to save her Jewish countrymen during the Nazi occupation of Holland. The fence protects it from the countless hands that unwittingly killed the previous tree by plucking its leaves in order to take a piece of her courage home. The well-intentioned visitors revere Corrie as a woman of strength whose spiritual stature grew during the duress of her imprisonment in the Ravensbruck concentration camp.

Forced to strip naked, face the jeers of leering Nazi soldiers, sleep eight abreast in lice-laden beds, and labor with little food, Prisoner 66730 lost her name, her nation, her normal life. Yet, by relying on their heavenly Father, Corrie and her sister Betsie turned the women of Barracks 28 away from their anger and pointed them to the Lord. Fearful foreigners joined together to revere God in worship. In Corrie's words,

> They were services like no others, these times in Barracks 28. A single meeting night might include a recital of the Magnificat in Latin by a group of Roman Catholics, a whispered hymn by some Lutherans, and a sotto-voce chant by Eastern Orthodox women. With each moment the crowd around us would swell, packing the nearby platforms, hanging over the edges, until the high structures groaned and swayed.
>
> At last either Betsie or I would open the Bible. Because only the Hollanders could understand the Dutch text we would translate aloud in German. And then we would hear the life-giving words passed back along the aisles in French, Polish, Russian, Czech, back into Dutch. They were little previews of heaven, these evenings beneath the light bulb.[1]

1. Corrie ten Boom, with John and Elizabeth Sherrill, *The Hiding Place* (New York, N.Y.: Bantam Books, 1974), p. 201.

Though the women worried that their Nazi captors would discover the forbidden meetings, the guards seemed blind to the gatherings. Later, Corrie learned that they avoided her dormitory because of the lice. God used the biting bugs as guardians to protect His daughters!

After her sister died and Corrie was released from the prison camp, she returned to Holland alone to pursue her new mission of declaring to the nations that "there is no pit so deep that He is not deeper still."[2] Corrie's message rang true to her hearers because she endured the pit and emerged with an invincible faith in God, a trusting spirit, and a forgiving heart. Though her fall into the depths of despair could have crippled her, she allowed God to use it to make her footsteps firm.

Corrie's response to her twentieth-century captivity mirrored the response of the apostle Paul, a first-century prisoner for the Lord.

Afflicted for Christ

Like Corrie ten Boom, Paul could speak with authority because of the things he suffered for Christ's sake. He even defended himself with his wounds in Galatians 6:17:

> From now on let no one cause trouble for me, for I
> bear on my body the brand-marks of Jesus.

The term "brand-marks" comes from the Greek root *stizo*, which designates "a mark incised or punched (for recognition of ownership)." Paul's scars branded him as belonging to Jesus—every mark on his body carried Christ's name. Hateful mobs hurled rocks at him, fearful foes flogged him, bitter rivals beat him with rods.

Paul continued his litany of afflictions in his second letter to the Corinthians:

> For we do not want you to be unaware, brethren,
> of our affliction which came to us in Asia, that we
> were burdened excessively, beyond our strength, so
> that we despaired even of life. (2 Cor. 1:8)

Despair? For Paul? Yes, even as Corrie ten Boom sometimes feared that the concentration camp would be the end, so Paul could very humanly lose his grasp on hope in the midst of his anguish.

---

2. ten Boom, *The Hiding Place*, p. 218.

Fortunately, Paul's pit was not so deep that Jesus' love and light were not deeper still.

Responding in Trust

What Paul terms "affliction," we would call unbearable pressure—pressure from rejection, pressure from physical and emotional strain, pressure extreme enough to cause debilitating depression. Pressure that makes you long to die. Yes, Paul faced it too. Like the rest of us, he had times when throwing in the towel sounded better than finishing the fight well. Isn't it comforting to know that the man who exhorts us to finish well felt completely spent at times? When exhorting us to persevere, he had heard the quitter's call. But he refused to follow those wayward words. Instead, he heeded a divine voice.

He Trusted God Alone

Paul learned to let the affliction strengthen his trust in God alone:

> Indeed, we had the sentence of death within ourselves so that we would not trust in ourselves, but in God who raises the dead; who delivered us from so great a peril of death, and will deliver us, He on whom we have set our hope. And He will yet deliver us. (vv. 9–10)

Did you catch what he was saying? "We were as good as dead, but God raises the dead!" And notice the verb tenses Paul uses: He *delivered* us, He *will deliver* us, He *will yet deliver* us. Paul no longer centered on his circumstances but on the Lord's power to deliver him.

This challenges our human nature. We often view ourselves as being capable, competent, and confident. We want to handle things ourselves. But circumstances can easily go beyond our limited ability to handle them. When we're finally at the end of ourselves, then we can do what Paul did—look up. We can pray, "Lord, I'm incapable, I'm incompetent, I'm not confident in my ability to solve this problem. I trust You and You alone." Then we can watch how the Lord will deliver us. And we can have hope again. (For another example, note David's response to incredible distress in 1 Sam. 30:1–6.)

He Focused on Things Unseen

In chapter 4, Paul elaborated further on the struggles he had faced in serving Christ—but also on what he *hadn't* had to face:

> We are afflicted in every way, but not crushed; perplexed, but not despairing; persecuted, but not forsaken; struck down, but not destroyed. (2 Cor. 4:8–9)

You can sense his spiritual resilience, can't you? How did he gain such steadfastness and hope? By using his trials as reminders to focus on the glorious things we can't see—yet:

> Therefore we do not lose heart, but though our outer man is decaying, yet our inner man is being renewed day by day. For momentary, light affliction is producing for us an eternal weight of glory far beyond all comparison, *while we look not at the things which are seen,* but at the things which are not seen; for the things which are seen are temporal, but the things which are not seen are eternal. (vv. 16–18, emphasis added)

Focusing on the unseen takes practice. Betsie ten Boom taught her sister Corrie to do it in World War II's German death camps. When Corrie despaired over the filth and famine, Betsie showed her the vast number of women desperate to know the Lord. Corrie learned quickly. Soon she began to view being stripped naked in front of cruel strangers as an opportunity to identify with her Savior who hung bare on the cross. When Betsie died in prison, the Lord revealed to Corrie the vibrant Betsie of her youth rather than the gaunt, skeletal woman of Ravensbruck Camp. Corrie finally recognized that eternal eyes see beyond what we see (see also Heb. 11:27).

He Acknowledged His Weakness

Paul served steadfastly even through intense hardships, which he lists later in the same letter:

> I've worked much harder, been jailed more often, beaten up more times than I can count, and at death's door time after time. I've been flogged five times with the Jews' thirty-nine lashes, beaten by Roman rods three times, pummeled with rocks once. I've been shipwrecked three times, and immersed in the

open sea for a night and a day. In hard traveling year in and year out, I've had to ford rivers, fend off robbers, struggle with friends, struggle with foes. I've been at risk in the city, at risk in the country, endangered by desert sun and sea storm, and betrayed by those I thought were my brothers. I've known drudgery and hard labor, many a long and lonely night without sleep, many a missed meal, blasted by the cold, naked to the weather.

And that's not the half of it, when you throw in the daily pressures and anxieties of all the churches. (2 Cor. 11:23b–28 THE MESSAGE)[3]

And let's not forget the thorn in his flesh. An anguish so deep that he prayed three times for its removal (12:8). A weakness so strong that God left it in Paul so that he could learn that God's power would be perfected in his weakness (v. 9). The Hebrew of Hebrews, the apostle of apostles was also the weakest of the weak . . . *except in God's power.* Paul added:

Therefore I am well content with weaknesses, with insults, with distresses, with persecutions, with difficulties, for Christ's sake; for when I am weak, then I am strong. (v. 10)

Are you afflicted, buffeted by life's storms? Turn to the Lord and trust Him. He can bring you through. Are you feeling crushed, confused, beaten, depressed? Don't be consumed by your trials or zero in only on your troubles. Instead, focus on the unseen and the everlasting—"the eternal weight of glory." Are you feeling overwhelmed by what looks humanly impossible? Acknowledge your weakness and depend on God's strength. For when you are weak, then you are strong in the Lord.

---

3. Eugene H. Peterson, *The Message: The Bible in Contemporary Language* (Colorado Springs, Colo.: NavPress, 2002), p. 2109.

🖋 *Living Insights*

The apostle Paul survived his trials by trusting in God alone, keeping his focus on things unseen, and embracing his weakness so that he could receive God's strength. But what about those of us living in the twenty-first century? How do we depend on God alone? How do we learn to see the unseen? How do we admit our weaknesses in a culture that applauds strength?

The celebrated Scottish preacher James Stewart challenges us with the Gospel's countercultural values: "It is always upon human weakness and humiliation, not human strength and confidence, that God chooses to build His Kingdom; and that he can use us not merely in spite of our ordinariness and helplessness and disqualifying infirmities, but precisely because of them."[4]

In God We Trust

American dollar bills read "In God We Trust." Financial analysts warn us to diversify our investments as the economy continues its downturn and the market's highs and lows rival Disney World's best roller coaster.

In money matters, putting our financial nest eggs in several baskets shows wisdom. In life matters, however, placing our trust in anyone or anything besides God or along with God reveals our doubt in Him. His hands provide the only nest that can protect our futures.

In your life, are you trusting in something besides God or in addition to Him? What is it?

_____

_____

Why do the things you trust in seem more dependable than God?

_____

_____

---

4. James Stewart, as quoted by Charles R. Swindoll in *Paul: A Man of Grace and Grit* (Nashville, Tenn.: The W Publishing Group, 2002), p. 241.

What helps you trust God?

_____

_____

Do You See What He Sees?

A familiar Christmas song echoes, "Do you hear what I hear?" What if God changed the lyrics and asked you, "Do you see what I see?"

Are your eyes fixed on things above or on circumstantial things?

_____

_____

What one thing can you do to sharpen your focus this week?

_____

_____

Are You "The Weakest Link?"

The sarcastic host of this game show mocked her contestants for their weaknesses, but the Host of Heaven wants to strengthen our weak links through His grace. We gain His power when we acknowledge our limitations.

What are your strengths?

_____

_____

What are your weaknesses?

_____

_____

Why is it so much easier to rely on our strengths than to admit our weaknesses?

_____

_____

Questions for Group Discussion

1. What does our hesitancy to completely trust God reveal about our view of Him?

2. Would reevaluating our view of God help us depend on Him more?

3. How does what we worry about reveal the focus of our hearts?

4. If we changed our heart's focus, how would our perspectives change?

5. If God is our power, why do we so often try to walk in our human strength?

6. Name one weakness that you want God to carry in His strength. How will you place that weakness in His hands?

Chapter 17

THINKING AS PAUL THOUGHT

Selections from Acts 21–23

Have you ever flown across the country on a spring day? The plane seems to hang effortlessly in the air, and the sun weaves its gilded rays through the clouds. The sky outside wraps you in its blue cocoon. The steady hum in your ears lulls your worries away. Your eyes slip shut.

Kathunk! A bag breaks free from its overhead compartment and thuds to the ground. Your eyes pop open. Baby bottles roll down the aisle. A passenger shrieks as the plane bounces like a badly driven bumper car. Outside, your soothing blue sky has turned a looming gray. Electric lightning replaces the gilded rays of the sun. Your sense of security has disappeared. Your shoulders stiffen as you grip the armrests more tightly.

Why are you afraid? Because you imagine that the plane might not make it through the storm. Though you've flown through turbulence before, your emotions push you to panic. How can you regain control of your fears?

By reminding yourself that the weather may have turned, but the pilot has not parachuted out. Just as he or she guided the plane through the calm, he or she can steer through the storm. The flight path may be bumpy, but the pilot knows the best way to get you back to earth.

So you have a choice: Will you lean on your fluctuating feelings? Or will you stand on your clear thinking?

We have the same choice to make in our lives. Our feelings are important, but they're not always accurate. We need to balance them with clear thought if we want to live wisely. This is especially true in the realm of our faith. In order to live effectively for Christ, we must think well.

Are you a clear thinker? Do your decisions point others to the Pilot of your spiritual plane? Could you convince a friend that your God can carry him or her through the struggles of life? Could you confidently explain to a coworker the hope that you have in Christ?

If you need to grow in this area, as many of us do, then the apostle Paul is the ideal mentor for you. He kept his mind clear and his Lord uppermost in his thoughts in the face of tremendous opposition. Let's return to Acts to learn from Paul's example.

Paul's Final Missionary Journey

On Paul's third missionary journey, he ministered in Galatia and Phrygia before traveling to Ephesus. In Ephesus, he found twelve disciples who needed further instruction in spiritual matters. After Paul baptized them in Jesus' name, he laid hands on them and they received the Holy Spirit. For three months, he proclaimed the truth boldly in the city's synagogue. However, when those who heard him hardened their hearts, he took the disciples with him and started teaching daily at the school of Tyrannus.

During the next two to three years, both the Jews and the Greeks in Asia heard the word of the Lord. Paul manifested God's power so strongly that handkerchiefs and aprons he touched healed people. Many sorcerers turned away from their magic. But silversmiths who crafted idols feared that Paul would put them out of business. Afraid that his message could close their shops and the grand temple of Artemis, they grabbed two of Paul's traveling companions and incited the people of Ephesus to revolt against them.

After officials quelled the riot, Paul proceeded to Macedonia and Achaia in Greece. When three months passed, he sailed to Troas via Macedonia to avoid a group of Jews who were plotting his assassination. At a midnight meeting in Troas, Paul brought a boy named Eutychus back to life after he drifted to sleep and fell from an upstairs window.

Paul continued to Assos by foot where he joined his fellow travelers on a ship bound for Caesarea. On the way to Caesarea, they stopped at Chios, Samos, and Miletus. In Miletus, Paul exhorted the Ephesian elders to continue the work of God and told them good-bye for the last time. From Miletus, he sailed to Tyre where he greeted more believers. Finally, he arrived in Caesarea, visited Philip, and proceeded to Jerusalem.

Clear Thinking in Tumultuous Times

Our times demand clear thinking. We live in a society whose members mold truth like play-dough. Some people perform magic tricks to try to make the line between right and wrong disappear. Others change their standards depending on what mood they're in.

In his day, Paul did not treat truth as a game. He knew that only clear, straight thinking would guide him through the difficult days ahead.

What specific challenges did Paul face? His return to Jerusalem after his third missionary journey precipitated a storm of persecution but also gave him new platforms from which to proclaim the Gospel of Jesus Christ. These included:

- His defense before a Temple mob in Jerusalem (Acts 21:40–22:21)

- His defense before the Sanhedrin Council in Jerusalem (Acts 23:1–6)

- His defense before Felix in Caesarea (Acts 24:10–21)

- His defense before Festus in Caesarea (Acts 25:8–11)

- His defense before Agrippa in Caesarea (Acts 26:2–29)

In this chapter, we'll study how Paul handled his first two defenses in Jerusalem. We'll cover his last three defenses in later chapters.

Paul's Arrest at the Temple in Jerusalem

Back in Jerusalem, Paul greeted his brothers and sisters in Christ, and they welcomed him. Together they praised God as Paul recounted "the things which God had done among the Gentiles through his ministry" (Acts 21:19). However, according to Luke, their reunion came to an abrupt close: "When the seven days were almost over, the Jews from Asia, upon seeing him in the temple, began to stir up all the crowd and laid hands on him" (v. 27).

From Asia all the way to Jerusalem, these enemies of the Gospel tracked Paul in order to kill him. They shouted,

> "Men of Israel, come to our aid! This is the man who preaches to all men everywhere against our people and the Law and this place; and besides he has even brought Greeks into the temple and has defiled this holy place." For they had previously seen Trophimus the Ephesian in the city with him, and they supposed that Paul had brought him into the temple. (vv. 28–29)

144

Hurling false accusations, they fired up the crowd and incited a riot. The mob roared. Paul writhed. As fists pounded him, he struggled to stay conscious. The commander of the Roman battalion soon heard that "all Jerusalem was in confusion" (v. 31). That news unnerved him, and springing to action to restore peace to his province, the commander ordered his men to charge into the center of the chaos—and to Paul.

Hundreds of uniformed officials on horses tend to have a calming effect on a crowd. The rioters receded, and Paul was rescued from being beaten to death. Remarkably, he asked permission to speak to the murderous mob. Would they listen? Paul would try, even showing them respect by speaking to them in their own language.

Paul's Defense before the Temple Mob

"Brethren and fathers, hear my defense which I now offer to you."

And when they heard that he was addressing them in the Hebrew dialect, they became even more quiet; and he said,

"I am a Jew, born in Tarsus of Cilicia, but brought up in this city, educated under Gamaliel, strictly according to the law of our fathers, being zealous for God just as you all are today. I persecuted this Way to the death, binding and putting both men and women into prisons, as also the high priest and all the Council of the elders can testify. From them I also received letters to the brethren, and started off for Damascus in order to bring even those who were there to Jerusalem as prisoners to be punished." (22:1–5)

Notice how Paul identified with his persecutors: speaking their common language, emphasizing "our fathers," and linking their zeal with his own. Then Paul explained how he changed and embraced the Way, telling both his conversion story (vv. 6–13) and God's new plan for him:

"And [Ananias] said [to me], 'The God of our fathers has appointed you to know His will and to see the Righteous One and to hear an utterance from His mouth. For you will be a witness for Him to all men of what you have seen and heard. Now why do you delay? Get up and be baptized, and wash away your sins, calling on His name.'

"It happened when I returned to Jerusalem and was praying in the temple, that I fell into a trance, and I saw Him saying to me, 'Make haste, and get out of Jerusalem quickly, because they will not accept your testimony about Me.' And I said, 'Lord, they themselves understand that in one synagogue after another I used to imprison and beat those who believed in You. And when the blood of Your witness Stephen was being shed, I also was standing by approving, and watching out for the coats of those who were slaying him.' And He said to me, 'Go! For I will send you far away to the Gentiles.'" (vv. 14–21)

Stop the chariot. He just used the G-word. Gentiles! BOOM! The crowd exploded. "He's not one of us. We don't talk to those dogs! Shut him up." Their rumbling rose to a roar.

The commander stepped between Paul and the crowd a second time. This time he took action. One of his centurions stretched Paul over a stump, bound his wrists and ankles with leather thongs, and raised the strap to whip him into submission. Just before the bone edges tore into Paul's flesh, he keenly questioned,

"Is it lawful for you to scourge a man who is a Roman and uncondemned?" (v. 25)

A Roman citizen?! The centurion dropped the whip. Under Roman law, he couldn't scourge a citizen without a trial. If he did, he could face the death penalty. So he untied Paul and released him (vv. 29–30). Even through the shouts and the shackles, Paul showed clear thinking. He knew that his rights as a Roman-born citizen guaranteed a hearing before the Roman court. There he would have another opportunity to speak of Christ—even amidst unfair treatment.

Paul's Defense before the Sanhedrin

In Acts 23, Paul appeared before the Jewish Supreme Court, the Sanhedrin. Here violence replaced justice, and even Paul briefly lost his cool:

Paul, looking intently at the Council, said,

> "Brethren, I have lived my life with a perfectly good conscience before God up to this day." The high priest Ananias commanded those standing beside him to strike him on the mouth. Then Paul said to him, "God is going to strike you, you whitewashed wall! Do you sit to try me according to the Law, and in violation of the Law order me to be struck?" But the bystanders said, "Do you revile God's high priest?" And Paul said, "I was not aware, brethren, that he was high priest; for it is written, 'You shall not speak evil of a ruler of your people.'" (23:1–5)

Whap! Paul's lip ballooned from the sudden wallop. He snapped back at Ananias's mock justice, "God is going to strike you, you whitewashed wall!" Because he did not know that Ananias was a high priest, Paul had unwittingly rebuked his ruler. By quickly quoting Exodus in recognition of his wrongdoing, Paul made amends for his untamed tongue.

Paul's unwavering wit won again when he turned the trial into a theological debate between the Sadducees and the Pharisees.

> But perceiving that one group were Sadducees and the other Pharisees, Paul began crying out in the Council, "Brethren, I am a Pharisee, a son of Pharisees; I am on trial for the hope and resurrection of the dead!" As he said this, there occurred a dissension between the Pharisees and Sadducees, and the assembly was divided. (vv. 6–7)

While the Sadducees denied resurrection, the Pharisees believed in it. According to verse 8, "The Sadducees say that there is no resurrection, nor an angel, nor a spirit, but the Pharisees acknowledge them all." The uproar that followed forced the Roman commander to pluck Paul out of harm's hands a third time.

God's Promise of Protection

Fearing that Paul would be torn to pieces by the angry religious parties, the commander ordered the troops to take Paul to the barracks. Alone in the dark night, Paul might have pondered, "What's the point of all of this? Every time I proclaim the truth, I become the town punching bag." He still felt their fists on his face, still tasted the blood in his mouth. He closed his eyes wearily.

147

But on the night immediately following, the Lord stood at his side and said, "Take courage; for as you have solemnly witnessed to My cause at Jerusalem, so you must witness at Rome also" (v. 11).

Paul looked at the Lord standing at his side and marveled at his Maker's promised protection. In the midst of terrible trials, God gave the suffering apostle the peace of His presence and a haven of hope. Paul slept, certain that he was headed to Rome on a divine assignment.

An Unlikely Hero

But while Paul slumbered, his enemies honed in. The next morning, forty conspirators vowed to murder him before breakfast.

> When it was day, the Jews formed a conspiracy and bound themselves under an oath, saying that they would neither eat nor drink until they had killed Paul. There were more than forty who formed this plot. They came to the chief priests and the elders and said, "We have bound ourselves under a solemn oath to taste nothing until we have killed Paul. Now therefore, you and the Council notify the commander to bring him down to you, as though you were going to determine his case by a more thorough investigation; and we for our part are ready to slay him before he comes near the place."
>
> But the son of Paul's sister heard of their ambush, and he came and entered the barracks and told Paul. Paul called one of the centurions to him and said, "Lead this young man to the commander, for he has something to report to him." (vv. 12–17)

Not one assassin, but forty of them. Forty terrorists with a secret sinister scheme: Ambush the apostle. But God had an undercover agent. Who? The little known, but very important nephew. Paul's sister's son stepped out of nowhere into the makings of a murderous plot. The Lord placed Paul's relative in the right place at the right time for His own righteous purpose—protecting Paul. After exposing the plan to Paul, the young man warned the Roman commander.

Yet again, the commander found himself surrounded by social upheaval. He wasted no time creating a plan to foil the scheme of the bloodthirsty bunch.

So the commander let the young man [Paul's nephew] go, instructing him, "Tell no one that you have notified me of these things." And he called to him two of the centurions and said, "Get two hundred soldiers ready by the third hour of the night to proceed to Caesarea, with seventy horsemen and two hundred spearmen." They were also to provide mounts to put Paul on and bring him safely to Felix the governor. (vv. 22–24)

Let's see—two hundred soldiers, two hundred spearmen, seventy horsemen, two centurions—that's four hundred seventy-two bodyguards for Paul. Roughly, eleven-and-a-half to one odds against the conspirators. Clearly, these hit men missed their mark. Paul and his enormous entourage arrived in Rome unscathed.

No matter how severe your situation, never bet against God. He stands in your darkness. He tastes your pain. He carries your future. Rely on Him to deliver you. Remember Paul's clear, focused thinking? He fixed his mind on the protection God promised—not the demise others threatened. When you feel fearful, focus your mind on the Father's secure promises. Your emotions may bounce in the turbulence, but your faith will keep you steady on God's course.

Living Insights

How do you respond to tumultuous times? Do you quiver when your circumstances shift? Or do you rest in the certainty that your God reigns even in the storm? Do your fears become all you see, or are you able to keep focused on Christ and His calling on your life? Psalm 46:1–3 reads,

> God is our refuge and strength,
> A very present help in trouble.
> Therefore we will not fear, though the earth should change
> And though the mountains slip into the heart of the sea;
> Though its waters roar and foam,
> Though the mountains quake at its swelling pride.

The psalmist assures us that God is our hiding place in times of trouble. Like Paul, when our world quakes and crumbles, we must use our heads. Fickle feelings lure us to doubt. Clear thinking leads us to trust.

What storms are you facing today?

_____

_____

_____

_____

What are your feelings about your circumstances?

_____

_____

_____

_____

How does the truth of Psalm 46 affect your outlook on the situation?

_____

_____

_____

_____

How can you think straight when your feelings tell you everything is out of control?

_____

_____

_____

_____

How does memorizing Scripture help you trust God rather than following your feelings?

_____

_____

_____

_____

What verse can you find to help you think straight the next time you feel out of control?

_____

_____

_____

Questions for Group Discussion

1. How do circumstances impact your thinking? Your faith?

2. What happens when your circumstances shift?

3. How can you move from your feelings to clear thinking?

4. Should you set aside your feelings altogether? How can you blend your feelings with straight thinking?

5. Why is it sometimes easier to trust your feelings over God's promises?

6. The next time your feelings contradict God's promises, how will you remind yourself to trust the truth?

Chapter 18

DEALING WITH CRITICS
AS PAUL DID
Acts 24:1–16; 25:1–12

S ticks and stones may break my bones, but words will never hurt me." How nice it would be if this childhood chant were true! Think back to your elementary school days. You may remember Butch the Bully hollering, "Hey, Fat-so!" Or Peggy Popular sneering, "You can't sit here, Four-Eyes." Chances are, you can still recount every juvenile jeer. Why? Because an ill-spoken word scars the heart more than a jagged stick or a hardened stone ever could.

And what about yesterday when Mr. Do-It-Right did you wrong? Even in adulthood, negative criticism cuts us to the core. We can't count on it going away, for it has been said, "Our Lord was nailed to a cross; so you can count on being nailed to the wall."[1] But we can seek truths from God's Word on how we should respond. Before we look at negative criticism in the life of the apostle Paul, let's examine some basic truths about it and its effects.

Four Spiritual Flaws of Negative Criticism

In *A Burden Shared*, David Roper accurately observed four spiritual truths about criticism. His observations could be called the Four Spiritual Flaws of Negative Criticism.[2]

First, *criticism always comes when we least need it*. Negative feedback never seems to come when we're on top of our game, but when we've dropped the ball and are lying at the bottom of the heap. After we've blown it and we're on our backs, some well-meaning brother or sister points out our fumbles just to "encourage" our Christian growth.

Second, *criticism seems to come when we least deserve it*. After an innocent mistake or an off-the-cuff comment, a Christian cohort

---

1. Unnamed author, as quoted by Charles R. Swindoll in *Paul: A Man of Grace and Grit* (Nashville, Tenn.: The W Publishing Group, 2002), p. 260.

2. The following four points are taken from David Roper's *A Burden Shared*, as quoted by Charles R. Swindoll in *Paul*, p. 261.

with the gift of criticism blasts us with bombs they call "constructive criticism." The funny thing is, it feels more like destructive dynamite.

Third, *criticism comes from people who are least qualified to give it.* Whose constructive criticism should we solicit? Those who know us best, who have walked with us in relationship, and who know both our beauty and our beast. Not strangers who only think they've read our story.

The reverse is also true: If we're getting ready to criticize someone that we don't know well, we need to stop. Loving someone begins with really knowing them. In the words of Proverbs 27:6a, "Faithful are the wounds of a friend." The Hebrew words paint a more vivid picture: "Faithful are bruises caused by the wounding of one who loves you." If we criticize someone we don't know deeply, our words will leave them feeling the bruise's ache without love's tenderness.

Fourth, *criticism frequently comes in a form that is least helpful to us.* Sometimes the advice is anything but friendly. Words laced with anger, jealousy, or rage reveal a lack of love and an absence of grace. Often these messages explode with emotion, but end anonymously. The sender has the gall to spew insults without the guts to sign his or her name. Such cruel cowardice demands that the receiver cultivate a tough hide. We, like Paul, must face our critics with grace and determined grit.

A Long Line of Constant Critics

From the moment he stepped into ministry, Paul's enemies trailed him like hounds. From Jerusalem to Antioch and back again, they tracked him so fervently that he seldom rested outside the range of their bellows. As the years passed, they persistently pursued. Remember Paul's words to the Corinthians, "For a wide door for effective service has opened to me, and *there are many adversaries*" (1 Cor. 16:9, emphasis added).

In Acts 24 and 25, Paul's third missionary journey had come to an end. But in his golden years as a missionary, he didn't get a gold watch. No winters at the fishing resort, no reverence for this weary workman. Instead, this tenderhearted missionary had to toughen his hide.

Beaten, mistreated, maligned, and misrepresented, Paul had gone where no tourist would ever venture. And he had set a course no novice would follow. Finally, he returned to Jerusalem. But before he could rest or reunite with his friends, a group of rabble-rousing

Jews hounded him. These Jews didn't even live in Jerusalem. They came all the way from Asia, determined to destroy him.

To avert an ambush and prevent mob violence from breaking out in the streets, the Roman guard ushered Paul out of Jerusalem to the Roman port city of Caesarea. There Paul found himself in court before Felix,[3] the governor of Judea:

> After five days the high priest Ananias came down with some elders, with an attorney named Tertullus, and they brought charges to the governor against Paul. After Paul had been summoned, Tertullus began to accuse him, saying to the governor, ". . . most excellent Felix, with all thankfulness . . . I beg you to grant us, by your kindness, a brief hearing. For we have found this man a real pest and a fellow who stirs up dissension among all the Jews throughout the world, and a ringleader of the sect of the Nazarenes. And he even tried to desecrate the temple; and then we arrested him." (Acts 24:1–6)

When someone lays on the flattery that thick in Texas, we call it "blowing smoke"! Tertullus, the tubby toga-wearing courtroom crook who had been bribed by conspirators, strutted onto the scene with no hard case. His words filled the room with hazy half-truths and distorted deceptions. John Pollock writes, "Tertullus puffed out his cheeks and hitched his robes in the immemorial manner of advocates with weak cases."[4]

Tertullus accused Paul of stirring up dissension, of being a ringleader of a sect of heretics, and of trying to desecrate the temple. He even told Felix, "We wanted to judge [Paul] according to our own Law. But Lysias the commander came along, and with much violence took him out of our hands, ordering his accusers to come before you" (vv. 6–8). But we know from Acts 23:27 that Lysias, the Roman commander, never used violence when he apprehended Paul—he used his guard to keep peace and to protect his prisoner from a murderous plot.

3. Felix assumed the role of Roman procurator of Judea after Pontius Pilate's death. Felix's time in power brought no more justice than before. With the exception of hearing Paul's case, Felix's career as governor faded into obscurity. His trials mocked justice and encouraged unfounded criticism against the accused.

4. John Pollock, *The Apostle: A Life of Paul* (Colorado Springs, Colo.: Cook Communications Ministries, 1985), p. 261.

Tertullus's show was a sham! And Paul knew it. He stood in the middle of the smoke and mirrors, calmly waiting for the appropriate time to clear the air.

Seven How-To's for Handling Constant Criticism

Paul's defense needed no extra eloquence. He spoke directly to the point, modeling a right response to constant criticism.

First, *he refused to be caught up in the emotion of the charges.* Paul opened with bold words:

> "Knowing that for many years you have been a judge to this nation, I cheerfully make my defense . . ." (24:10)

Cheerfully? Didn't he mean to say bitterly? Angrily? Hostilely? They'd hurled untrue accusations at him, calling him a pest and a temple-trasher. But Paul refused to let his emotions rule his reason.

Second, *he stayed with the facts.*

> ". . . since you can take note of the fact that no more than twelve days ago I went up to Jerusalem to worship. Neither in the temple, nor in the synagogues, nor in the city itself did they find me carrying on a discussion with anyone or causing a riot." (vv. 11–12)

Paul challenged them to check his record. He directly addressed the specific charges. Yes, he was at the temple, but no desecration took place. No riot broke out. Paul's clear, direct communication bolstered his credibility in the eyes of the court.

Third, *he told the truth with a clear conscience.*

> "Nor can they prove to you the charges of which they now accuse me. But this I admit to you, that according to the Way which they call a sect I do serve the God of our fathers, believing everything that is in accordance with the Law and that is written in the Prophets; having a hope in God, which these men cherish themselves, that there shall certainly be a resurrection of both the righteous and the wicked. In view of this, I also do my best to maintain always a blameless conscience both before God and before men." (vv. 13–16)

Paul showed his audience that he had integrity and credibility. He shared their beliefs. He followed the God of their fathers. His message carried weight!

One thing to note here: Always avoid falsehoods when making a defense. As soon as you step into a lie, you weaken your case. If you have crossed the line between truth and falsehood, go back. Admit it. Correct it. Don't use lies to support your cause. Go with the truth every time. Paul told the truth with a clear conscience, and his clarity made his opponents nervous.

Fourth, *he identified the original source of the criticism.*

> "Now after several years I came to bring alms to my nation and to present offerings; in which they found me occupied in the temple, having been purified, without any crowd or uproar. But there were some Jews from Asia—who ought to have been present before you and to make accusation, if they should have anything against me." (vv. 17–19)

Paul knew the root of the grapevine. His present accusers were only secondary informants. The star witnesses in his case weren't eyewitnesses at all. They based their stories on hearsay and their own imaginations.

Fighting invisible critics fuels futility. Original roots can do damage, but usually it's the grapevine growing wild that strangles the truth. Paul dealt directly with the original source.

Fifth, *he would not surrender and quit.*

> "Or else let these men themselves tell what misdeed they found when I stood before the Council . . ." (v. 20)

Paul wanted his accusers to name his crime. They had followed him. He hadn't run. They had beaten him. He hadn't given up. They had accused him. He had stood firm in the truth. Now he wanted them to take responsibility for their actions. He let the Lord carry him through the worst they could dish out.

Faced with Tertullus's obvious fiction, Felix fidgeted. He couldn't condemn Paul because the facts were in Paul's favor. Yet he couldn't release Paul because of public pressure. Rather than ruling with authority, he weaseled out by declaring a recess. For two years, Paul was left in confinement. And for two years, Paul persevered, waiting to plead his case to the man who would not hear and who refused to act.

Sixth, *he did not become impatient or bitter.* Two years crept by, but no one heard Paul's case. Neither convicted nor acquitted, he served countless hours for an imaginary crime.

Then, the conspirators again planned to ambush Paul (25:1–3). They went right back to court with the same unfair, inaccurate accusations (vv. 6–7). Commence round two. But now Festus, rather than Felix, ruled the court. This time, Paul condensed his defense into nineteen English words: "I have committed no offense either against the Law of the Jews or against the temple or against Caesar" (v. 8). No venom of bitterness, outrage, or panic here. The brevity of Paul's words revealed the peace he felt even in the midst of an unjust imprisonment. He refused to let his emotions override his trust in God's promise to take him to Rome.

Last, *he stood on the promise of God.* Paul made it through two years of unjust imprisonment and two false trials by holding on to God's faithful promise from Acts 23:11: "Take courage; for as you have solemnly witnessed to My cause at Jerusalem, so you must witness at Rome also." He knew that God had ordained the kangaroo courts so that he could proclaim the message of Christ. His ticket to Caesarea ultimately took him to court in Rome. Why was it important that Paul witness in Rome? Because Rome was the political and cultural center of the first-century world. As a result of Paul's imprisonment and his bold response to his critics, the Gospel would echo in the ears of four politicians—Felix, Festus, Agrippa, and also Rome's ruler, Nero.

Even when he faced evil opponents and unfair imprisonment, Paul proved himself God-centered rather than self-centered. The next time unqualified critics hurl their wounding words when you least need it and when you don't deserve it, copy Paul's pattern:

- Refuse to get caught up in the emotion of the charges.

- Stay with the facts.

- Tell the truth with a clear conscience.

- Identify the original source of the accusations.

- Don't surrender or quit.

- Don't become impatient or bitter.

- Stand firm on the promises of God.

Although you can't stop the critics from hurling their stones, you can control your reaction to the wounds. A poor reaction will fuel their fire, but a wise response will quench their flames.

✒ *Living Insights*

If we want to avoid getting caught up in our emotions when our critics accuse us, we need to consider how to express our emotions in a way that pleases God. What does the Lord say about the emotion of *anxiety?* Philippians 4:6–7 says:

> Be anxious for nothing, but in everything by prayer and supplication with thanksgiving let your requests be made known to God. And the peace of God, which surpasses all comprehension, will guard your hearts and your minds in Christ Jesus.

According to God's Word, what are we to worry, or be anxious, about?

_____

When we are worried, what are we to do?

_____

How are we to do it?

_____

If we do it, what is God's promise to us?

_____

_____

_____

How powerful is the Lord? How powerful is His peace?

_____

Is the problem you are worried about stronger than God? Greater than Jesus?

_____

Using your Bible's index or concordance, look up other emotions you face, and find verses that will help you express those feelings well.

What verses did you find on *anger?*

_____

_____

_____

_____

What verses did you find on *sadness?*

_____

_____

_____

_____

What verses did you find on *other emotions?*

_____

_____

_____

_____

_____

_____

_____

_____

_____

 *Questions for Group Discussion*

1. God calls us to walk through life with a clear conscience. What should we do if we find ourselves being dishonest in a situation?

2. How can you receive an apology for a lie in a way that encourages the person to not be dishonest again?

3. How do you trust someone who has deceived you in the past?

4. When you are wounded by the words of another, with how many people do you share your hurt before you go to the source? If the situation were reversed, would you want the person who was hurt by you to tell that same number of people before they told you? How does telling too many people about a hurtful situation feed the grapevine?

5. When you are wounded by others' careless words, what emotions do you feel? How can you express your emotions without letting them seethe into sinful responses?

Chapter 19

STANDING TALL AS PAUL STOOD

Acts 25:13–26:32

The 1998 movie *Simon Birch* tells the story of a boy hero who stood tall even though he was less than three feet high. This child with stunted growth faced his family's rejection and his culture's disdain. But Simon believed that despite his disability, God had called him to a special purpose. He challenged a church to change and ultimately proved that his small size never limited his brave heart.

When the church bus plummeted into a local lake, Simon took the initiative to direct his peers to safety. After leading the other children safely to the shore, he dove back into the icy water to free the last child's stuck foot. His size allowed him to maneuver in the tight space under the bus seat. God had specially designed his diminutive frame and his courageous spirit for this very day. By responding to a terrifying accident with selfless action, Simon ultimately saved his friends.

Like Simon Birch, real-life heroes—men and women who stand tall and refuse to shrink from difficult situations—have stories that follow a pattern. It usually goes something like this:

First, *there's something wrong on the cultural scene.* A cultural force that threatens well-being must be challenged.

Second, *there's a principle at stake.* A fundamental value is being sacrificed to that cultural force.

Third, *there's an element of risk involved.* In addition to risking personal safety, a hero faces being misunderstood, misrepresented, maligned, or mistreated. However, ignoring the problem makes matters worse. Taking a risk and doing something heroic may mean acting alone or joining the minority.

Standing as History's Heroes Stood

History proves that most heroes stand alone. William Wilberforce stood against slavery and voted against his fellow British Parliament members who supported it. His outcry against the wrongs of slavery would not be heeded until after his death.

161

In America's early years, Patrick Henry cried, "Give me liberty or give me death!" in opposition to British tyranny. His fellow countrymen, who might have otherwise chosen to ignore the political problems, eventually called him a hero for preserving their way of life.

In the 1960s, Martin Luther King Jr. challenged the injustice of segregation when many wanted to fold their arms, look the other way, and pretend that the problem of racial prejudice didn't matter.

Early in this new millennium, Todd Beamer showed extraordinary courage by rallying his fellow passengers aboard Flight 93 to revolt against the September 11 hijackers. Although these men and women kept the plane from hitting its intended target, they could not prevent it from crashing into a Pennsylvania field. In the last moments of their lives, they acted courageously, trying to keep others from harm.

We can make two observations about heroes: First, *they don't usually seem like heroes at the time they act.* At the time most heroes act, others may view them as people who make unnecessary waves. Many visionaries were seen as shortsighted in their day. Only hindsight showed the heroism of their actions.

Second, *heroism is not genetic.* We'd like to think our children get their heroic traits from our superior genes. But heroism does not come from our bloodlines. It comes from following in line behind those who stood tall before us.

We can look to the heroes of the past as we choose our future actions. The Bible tells the stories of many of them, including the apostle Paul. Paul stood taller than most heroes. As you recall from Acts 25, Paul had endured four court trials. After being held under arrest for over two years, Paul faced his fifth trial—his final chance to proclaim the truth of Christ before being shipped to Rome. His defense in court showed his strength to stand alone when the majority stood against him.

Standing Respectfully before Immoral Authorities

After Paul's fourth trial, Festus needed a valid reason to bring Paul before the Emperor Nero, so he solicited the help of his neighbor, King Agrippa. Perhaps the king could concoct some credible evidence. As the curtain opens in Acts 25, King Agrippa enters.

> So, on the next day when Agrippa came together with Bernice amid great pomp, and entered the auditorium accompanied by the commanders and the

prominent men of the city, at the command of Festus, Paul was brought in. (v. 23)

Picture this as a better-than-Broadway drama with a few shady characters. At thirty-two years of age, King Agrippa had gained political power among the Jews. Before his death, King Agrippa's father, Herod I, tried to kill Peter. Agrippa's sisters, Drusilla and Bernice, earned notoriety in their own right. Drusilla left her husband to marry the same Felix who tried Paul. And Bernice indulged in an incestuous relationship with her brother, King Agrippa. The members of this crooked family tree set themselves up to judge Paul. As the trial opened, Festus actually admitted that he had no evidence:

> Festus said, "King Agrippa, and all you gentlemen here present with us, you see this man about whom all the people of the Jews appealed to me, both at Jerusalem and here, loudly declaring that he ought not to live any longer. But I found that he had committed nothing worthy of death; and since he himself appealed to the Emperor, I decided to send him. Yet I have nothing definite about him to write to my lord. Therefore I have brought him before you all and especially before you, King Agrippa, so that after the investigation has taken place, I may have something to write." (vv. 24–26)

When Paul was questioned, he spoke to this immoral clan with respect. He began his defense by addressing Agrippa courteously:

> "In regard to all the things of which I am accused by the Jews, I consider myself fortunate, King Agrippa, that I am about to make my defense before you today; especially because you are an expert in all customs and questions among the Jews; therefore I beg you to listen to me patiently." (Acts 26:2–3).

When Paul had the opportunity to stand tall and tell his story, he did it with class and dignity. He didn't blast these people for their morally messed-up lives. Instead, he considered it a privilege to stand before them. Take note: If you ever have the opportunity to speak with people of high rank or significant authority, treat them with respect. Though you may not agree with their lifestyle choices, realize that it is an honor to be heard. Carry that privilege carefully.

Paul then proceeded with his defense:

> "So then, all Jews know my manner of life from
> my youth up, which from the beginning was spent
> among my own nation and at Jerusalem; since they
> have known about me for a long time, if they are
> willing to testify, that I lived as a Pharisee according
> to the strictest sect of our religion. And now I am
> standing trial for the hope of the promise made by
> God to our fathers; the promise to which our twelve
> tribes hope to attain, as they earnestly serve God
> night and day. And for this hope, O King, I am being
> accused by Jews." (vv. 4–7)

Perhaps Paul envisioned the faces of his peers. He recounted
his life as an open book—his schooling in Jerusalem, his previous
piety as a Pharisee, and his hope in his Messiah. That hope led
Paul to believe that the crucified One could be raised from the
dead. So he asked in verse 8, "Why is it considered incredible among
you people if God does raise the dead?"

As Agrippa listened, Paul continued to explain the way he
persecuted Christians when he followed the Pharisees. He set forth
an honest, unguarded set of six admissions:

> "So then, I thought to myself that I had to do
> many things hostile to the name of Jesus of Nazareth.
> And this is just what I did in Jerusalem; not only
> did [1] I lock up many of the saints in prisons, having
> received authority from the chief priests, but also
> when they were being put to death [2] I cast my vote
> against them. And as [3] I punished them often in all
> the synagogues, [4] I tried to force them to blaspheme;
> and [5] being furiously enraged at them, [6] I kept
> pursuing them even to foreign cities." (vv. 9–11)

But Paul's persecuting ceased when the Lord confronted him
on the road to Damascus.

> "While so engaged as I was journeying to Dam-
> ascus with the authority and commission of the chief
> priests, at midday, O King, I saw on the way a light
> from heaven, brighter than the sun, shining all
> around me and those who were journeying with me.

164

And when we had all fallen to the ground, I heard a voice saying to me in the Hebrew dialect, 'Saul, Saul, why are you persecuting Me? It is hard for you to kick against the goads.'" (vv. 12–14)

By telling Paul to stop "kick[ing] against the goads," the Lord challenged him to stop fighting against Him. Then He revealed Himself and His plan to Paul.

"And I said, 'Who are you Lord?' And the Lord said, 'I am Jesus whom you are persecuting. But get up and stand on your feet; for this purpose I have appeared to you, to appoint you a minister and a witness not only to the things which you have seen, but also to the things in which I will appear to you; rescuing you from the Jewish people and from the Gentiles, to whom I am sending you, to open their eyes so that they may turn from darkness to light and from the dominion of Satan to God, that they may receive forgiveness of sins and an inheritance among those who have been sanctified by faith in Me.'" (vv. 15–18)

The Lord called Paul to stop mistreating Christians and to serve as His messenger to the Jews and the Gentiles. Paul obeyed. And that's why the Jews wanted him dead. They didn't like his claim that Jesus was the Messiah. But Paul stood up under their persecution and continued to proclaim the truth:

"So, King Agrippa, I did not prove disobedient to the heavenly vision, but kept declaring both to those of Damascus first, and also at Jerusalem and then throughout all the region of Judea, and even to the Gentiles, that they should repent and turn to God, performing deeds appropriate to repentance. For this reason some Jews seized me in the temple and tried to put me to death. So, having obtained help from God, I stand to this day testifying both to small and great, stating nothing but what the Prophets and Moses said was going to take place; that the Christ was to suffer, and that by reason of His resurrection from the dead He would be the first to proclaim light both to the Jewish people and to the Gentiles." (vv. 19–23)

"Stop!" Festus screamed upon hearing Paul's assertion that Christ was the Messiah and fit the pattern of the Holy Scriptures. He accused Paul of madness.

> While Paul was saying this in his defense, Festus said in a loud voice, "Paul, you are out of your mind! Your great learning is driving you mad." (v. 24)

Paul did not miss a beat. He shifted the attendent from Festus's outcry to King Agrippa.

> Paul said, "I am not out of my mind, most excellent Festus, but I utter words of sober truth. For the king knows about these matters, and I speak to him also with confidence, since I am persuaded that none of these things escape his notice; for this has not been done in a corner. King Agrippa, do you believe the Prophets? I know that you do." (vv. 25–27)

Paul engaged the king not as a royal figure, but as a man in need of the Savior. His question compelled the king to consider his claims.

> Agrippa replied to Paul, "In a short time you will persuade me to become a Christian." (v. 28)

Paul hoped that everyone in the room would come to believe in Christ. He said,

> "I would wish to God, that whether in a short or long time, not only you, but also all who hear me this day, might become such as I am, except for these chains." (v. 29)

After hearing Paul's desire,

> The king stood up and the governor and Bernice, and those who were sitting with them, and when they had gone aside, they began talking to one another, saying, "This man is not doing anything worthy of death or imprisonment." And Agrippa said to Festus, "This man might have been set free if he had not appealed to Caesar." (vv. 30–32)

Paul's judges missed his message. Do you see the irony? The shackled man was free because he knew Christ, and those who held the power to release him from his shackles were prisoners to their sinful unbelief. Though Paul walked back to his cell in chains, he knew that his message would give him and those who believed it eternal freedom.

Standing Tall in Modern Times

We can take two truths from Paul's story. First, *when you choose to stand tall, you're so focused you feel invincible.* When you take the risk to take a stand, you're unconcerned about yourself, unimpressed with those in authority over you, unintimidated by fighting alone against the majority, and uninhibited in your zeal and determination. Most people never have the experience of soaring because they fear falling. Heroes are willing to risk.

Second, *after standing tall, you're often unaware of the impact you've made.* After his audience left, Paul didn't hear their conversations. Spending another routine day in his cell, he didn't witness the results of his words. Only God knows the impact His servants make. As His servants, we are to stand tall, leaving the results to Him.

William Wilberforce, Patrick Henry, and Martin Luther King Jr. are all names we've heard heralded in our history books. But before they faced the issues of slavery, unjust government, and racial discrimination, they lived ordinary lives.

After September 11, 2001, the name Todd Beamer echoed from our televisions. But on Monday, September 10, the New Jerseyan spent another workday doing out-of-town business. He was just like the rest of us—working to pay the bills and counting the hours until he would be home with his family. Like Wilberforce, Henry, and King, Beamer led a normal life until it was interrupted by a situation that demanded action. When challenged by evil, this everyday man fought back.

Although your day-to-day life probably won't be threatened by fanatical terrorists, you will face times when you need to stand tall for a cause that the crowd would rather ignore. When those days come, will you stand as Paul stood or will you sit in the crowd?

✒ _Living Insights_

Because of his eternal freedom, Paul could stand tall against his culture, saying what people needed to hear even when they didn't want to listen. But remember that while Paul was a hero, he didn't possess superhuman powers. He was merely a man who chose to rely on God's divine power to give him the courage to stand tall while those around him slouched.

What about you? Do you know the eternal freedom that Paul knew? Do you believe that Christ offered you eternal freedom by dying to pay for your sins and rising from the dead? Have you accepted His offer?

_____

_____

If you haven't yet accepted Christ's offer, you can do it now. He died to pay the debt for the things you have done wrong. He wants you to know Him as intimately as Paul did.

If you'd like to accept Christ's offer of eternal freedom, you can do so by praying this simple prayer or one like it:

> Heavenly Father,
> I am sorry for my sins. I believe that Jesus died on the cross to pay for my sins, and I accept the eternal freedom You are offering me now. Thank You. Amen.

If you're curious to know more about Christ, try reading the Gospel of John in the New Testament. Be sure to use a version of the Bible that is easy to understand, such as the New International Version (NIV).

If you have accepted Christ's offer, how can you challenge the people you interact with in your daily life to consider the claims of Christ?

_____

_____

_____

When the people around you follow cultural trends that threaten society's well-being, how can you stand up for your beliefs in a respectful way? How can you use your influence to turn the cultural tide toward a godly standard?

_____

_____

_____

Questions for Group Discussion

1. What fears lead you to play it safe rather than stand tall against harmful cultural trends?

2. What is the difference between boldly challenging our culture and offensively insulting our neighbors?

3. How can we challenge those who do not believe in Christ to consider the claims of His message in a way that will draw them to Him rather than repelling them?

4. If our lives do not match our words, what message will non-believers receive?

5. What are the motives of someone who stands tall for his or her own glory? Of someone who stands tall for God's glory?

6. What are your motives for standing tall?

Chapter 20

HOW TO HANDLE
A SHIPWRECK
Selections from Acts 27

On April 14, 1912, an iceberg tore the *Titanic* in two. Touted as a twentieth-century miracle, it was the largest ship ever to set sail. But it never saw its destination of New York. Instead, all 46,000 gross tons of the steamer reached the bottom of the Atlantic less than three hours after water started pouring through her gashed hull. Of the 2,220 passengers, only 1,530 survived.[1]

While you've probably heard the story of the *Titanic* many times, you may not be as familiar with another ship that ran aground. This first-century ship didn't carry millionaires, but a group of prisoners bound for Rome. Though their ship wrecked on the island of Malta in the Mediterranean Sea, this crew fared better than the *Titanic*'s ticket-holders. Just as God had promised, every one of them, including the apostle Paul, survived.

Unlike Paul and his shipmates on that fateful voyage, you're probably not wet, cold, and seasick. As you read this chapter from your warm and comfortable chair, try to imagine the extreme circumstances Luke described as he, Paul, other prisoners, and the Roman guard set sail from Caesarea, a port city northwest of Jerusalem.

Setting Sail for Rome

What began as an innocuous trip to Rome turned into one of the most frightening experiences of the entire crew's lives. Luke provided an eyewitness account of the journey. He describes the scene as they set sail from Caesarea, encountered the fateful storm, and survived the dramatic shipwreck on the way to Rome. Luke's description was not meant to be a day-by-day account of the journey. Rather, his record reflects personal observations.

1. "*Titanic* Disaster," Microsoft® Encarta® Online Encyclopedia 2002 © 1997–2002 Microsoft Corporation. All rights reserved, available at http://encarta.msn.com.

All Aboard

Under the charge of the Roman centurion named Julius, Paul, Luke, and their Macedonian companion Aristarchus boarded a ship bound for Rome. A large merchant ship working along the southern coastline took them from Caesarea to Myra. At Myra, they changed ships and proceeded past Rhodes, then Crete, and were shipwrecked at the obscure island of Malta. After three months in Malta, they sailed past Sicily to the harbor near Rome.

The ancient vessels that carried Paul did not resemble our modern-day ships. Shaped nearly as squarely at the bow as at the stern, they lumbered on the sea. The single mast with one massive sail made the giant barges hard to maneuver even in calm waters. Tumultuous winds and choppy waters could split apart the timbers of the simple ships. Today, we wouldn't trust these wooden rafts to travel two miles. But in Paul's day, they provided the fastest route to Rome. Though he knew that he and his companions would arrive in Rome, Paul had no idea how circuitously he would get there.

The one-way cruise from Caesarea to Italy probably commenced in the transitional days of late August as summer gave way to fall. When chilly gales met balmy breezes, an unpredictable storm surged to full strength. Luke describes how its volatile force threatened the ship and her crew:

> When we had sailed slowly for a good many days, and with difficulty had arrived off Cnidus, since the wind did not permit us to go farther, we sailed under the shelter of Crete, off Salmone; and with difficulty sailing past it we came to a place called Fair Havens, near which was the city of Lasea.
>
> When considerable time had passed and the voyage was now dangerous, since even the fast was already over, Paul began to admonish them, and said to them, "Men, I perceive that the voyage will certainly be with damage and great loss, not only of the cargo and the ship, but also of our lives." But the centurion was more persuaded by the pilot and the captain of the ship than by what was being said by Paul. (Acts 27:7–11)

The centurion's choice to ignore Paul's advice cost the whole crew greatly. He left the ship vulnerable to the open sea's unpredictable moods. The difficult waters changed to dangerous waves in one night. Calm breezes became raging winds. As the gale howled and the sea tossed, everyone on the ship expected the worst. Luke recorded the gravity of their situation, "But before very long there rushed down from the land a violent wind, called Euraquilo; and when the ship was caught in it and could not face the wind, we gave way to it and let ourselves be driven along" (vv. 14–15).

Although we don't call them "Euraquilos," we are familiar with northeasters—"the combination of gale-force winds and rough seas that rage along the eastern seaboard from south to north, dumping heavy rain, snow, and ice along the way."[2] These blizzard conditions create hazards on land and wreak havoc over water.

In their desperation to survive the storm, the crew supported the ship with cables, anchored the boat, and threw cargo overboard (vv. 17–19). In addition to bringing icy rain, the clouds blocked the stars (v. 20). Without them, the captain could not navigate. As they drifted in the dark, their hearts sank as they faced being swallowed by the angry sea.

At midnight on the fourteenth day, the sailors' hearts leapt at the sight of land. But their excitement quickly turned to panic as they estimated the size of the land and realized the risk of running aground. In this dark hour of night, the edge of the shoreline loomed invisible under the water. They cast four anchors from the stern and longed for the light of dawn as the boat jerked against the sea (vv. 27–29).

But, as we will soon see, Paul stood up among them and said, "I urge you to keep up your courage" (v. 22). How do you keep it together when your life is splitting apart? Too often, when we face personal storms, we identify with the other 275 passengers rather than with Paul. Focusing on the wind rather than the One who controls it, we tend to hear the creaks and the groans of the ship rather than the assurance of God's Word. God yearns for us to listen to Him—to put our confidence in Him while the waves beat against our boat. If we put our faith in circumstances, our emotions will change with the wind. If we trust in Him, we can weather the most severe squall.

---

2. Charles R. Swindoll, *Paul: A Man of Grace and Grit* (Nashville, Tenn.: The W Publishing Group, 2002), p. 290.

Steadying Your Storm-Tossed Soul with Four Spiritual Anchors

When you face your storms, you'll need the following four anchors to keep you from losing sight of the One who will carry you through your despair. Notice the way Paul uses them in the events that followed.

First, you'll need the *anchor of stability*. What brings stability when life brings storms? Remembering the promises of God and the faithfulness of God. Paul was able to spur the men onward because he believed God would fulfill His promise.

> Since neither sun nor stars appeared for many days, and no small storm was assailing us, from then on all hope of our being saved was gradually abandoned.
>
> When they had gone a long time without food, then Paul stood up in their midst and said, "Men, you ought to have followed my advice and not to have set sail from Crete and incurred this damage and loss. Yet now I urge you to keep up your courage, for there will be no loss of life among you, but only of the ship. For this very night an angel of the God to whom I belong and whom I serve stood before me, saying, 'Do not be afraid, Paul; you must stand before Caesar; and behold, God has granted you all those who are sailing with you.' Therefore, keep up your courage, men, for I believe God that it will turn out exactly as I have been told. But we must run aground on a certain island." (vv. 20–26)

The anchor of stability holds firm when it's dark and you can't find your way out of the storm. Just when you want to abandon all hope of being saved, God exhorts you not to fear because He has a plan. When you face intense adversity, it's difficult to look beyond the crashing waves and blistering winds. But in the midst of his storm, Paul urged the men on his ship to keep up their courage because God had promised that though the ship would sink, they would all survive. He gauged his situation by the Word of God rather than by the force of the gale. No matter how hard the wind whips in your ears, don't let it keep you from listening to God's Word. The power of God's Word supersedes the strength of any wind.

Second, you'll need the *anchor of unity*.

> But when the fourteenth night came, as we were being driven about in the Adriatic Sea, about midnight the sailors began to surmise that they were approaching some land. They took soundings and found it to be twenty fathoms; and a little farther on they took another sounding and found it to be fifteen fathoms. Fearing that we might run aground somewhere on the rocks, they cast four anchors from the stern and wished for daybreak. But as the sailors were trying to escape from the ship and had let down the ship's boat into the sea, on the pretense of intending to lay out anchors from the bow, Paul said to the centurion and to the soldiers, "Unless these men remain in the ship, you yourselves cannot be saved." Then the soldiers cut away the ropes of the ship's boat and let it fall away. (vv. 27–32)

As the ship rocked violently on the waves, the crew's imaginations spun out of control. Men wanted to bail out and save themselves. Paul knew that the chaos of "every man for himself" would kill most of the crew. But if all of them would work together, they could all survive.

When your ship is about to sink, do you bail out or do you stay with your shipmates? As part of our human nature, we desire to be alone in a one-man dinghy—to retreat and tough it out by ourselves. But by alienating ourselves, we sink further into depression. Tragically, some of us are tempted to turn away from loved ones and drown our pain in a stranger's arms, the bottle's buzz, or a drug's haze. Others of us follow a more culturally accepted route by jumping into the depths of busyness to forget our sorrow. But escape isolates us—leaving us to battle the elements alone. Locking arms with other believers provides support when you feel like you bought a ticket on the *Titanic*. Stay with those who love you, and let God's lifeboat rescue all of you.

Third, you'll need the *anchor of renewal*.

> Until the day was about to dawn, Paul was encouraging them all to take some food, saying, "Today is the fourteenth day that you have been constantly watching and going without eating, having taken

nothing. Therefore I encourage you to take some food, for this is for your preservation, for not a hair from the head of any of you will perish." Having said this, he took bread and gave thanks to God in the presence of all, and he broke it and began to eat. All of them were encouraged and they themselves also took food. (vv. 33–36)

The passengers traveling with Paul were spent from exposure to the elements and a lack of food. Their physical resources were tapped out. Paul encouraged the men to renew themselves both physically and spiritually. He exhorted them to eat, but not before they prayed. Some of the men prayed that day for the first time in their lives. Hours before their ship sank, they learned to rely on God's power to restore their strength.

Though we're not lost at sea, we often feel that way. We run our tanks dry. Fighting our battles alone, we grow too weary to refuel. The anchor of renewal guards against that kind of physical and spiritual collapse.

Finally, when the hull of your ship rips open and water engulfs you, you'll need the *anchor of reality* to keep you alert and involved.

But striking a reef where two seas met, they ran the vessel aground; and the prow stuck fast and remained immovable, but the stern began to be broken up by the force of the waves. The soldiers' plan was to kill the prisoners, so that none of them would swim away and escape; but the centurion, wanting to bring Paul safely through, kept them from their intention, and commanded that those who could swim should jump overboard first and get to land, and the rest should follow, some on planks, and others on various things from the ship. And so it happened that they all were brought safely to land. (vv. 41–44)

The anchor of reality says, "Jump right in. Get directly involved. Don't be passive. Be engaged in the action."[3] For Paul and his companions, the message was "Swim to shore!" They had no other options. The Coast Guard wasn't coming. For them, S-O-S meant

3. Swindoll, *Paul*, p. 298.

Sink-Or-Swim. So all 276 of them swam. With such a high number of men, surely there were losses, right? But no, not even one. God keeps His promises every time. *He is faithful.*

Although God kept His Word, He didn't miraculously move the men to the island. He gave them the ability to get to shore safely, but they still had to swim. Everybody on the ship got to shore—but not before they got pounded by the rain and slapped by the surf. "All those going through a storm must be engaged in the process. No one is promised a magical escape clause. Passivity is faith's enemy."[4] Like Paul and his shipmates—you can survive your storm, but you can't avoid getting wet.

Living Insights

The secret of surviving a shipwreck lies in proper preparation and in banking on the promises of God. A sea captain never leaves the port without an anchor. How do you ensure that your spiritual anchors are ready for a storm?

Every one of God's promises is an anchor for stormy days. He filled the Bible with promises to His children. Read Isaiah 43:1–2. In these verses, your Father gave you another anchor to hold you steady.

What does the Lord tell Jacob?

How does the Lord's role as your Creator give Him the credibility to tell you not to fear?

If you are a believer, how does the fact that God has redeemed you prove that He will deliver you from life's storms?

4. Swindoll, *Paul*, p. 298.

_____

_____

God calls you "His." How does it make you feel? As His child, how much does He value you?

_____

_____

_____

How will God's promise that He will be with you through the waters change the way you'll respond to your next storm? Memorize God's promise so that, like Paul, you'll remember it when the sea churns and the wind howls.

_____

_____

_____

Questions for Group Discussion

1. What type of storms make you want to isolate yourself from other Christ-followers? When you isolate yourself, how do you cope with your pain?

2. How can you establish accountability with two to three Christian friends so that they won't let you escape to your one-man dinghy when you're in a storm?

3. When your friends try to keep you on the boat, do you usually fight them? If so, how can you change your response?

4. Do you ever let your physical or spiritual tank run dry? How do you react to life's storms when your gauge reads empty? How can you make sure that your tank gets filled before you need a tow truck?

5. When facing your storm, do you swim to shore or let the current pull you under? If you feel caught in the undertow right now, how can you improve your stroke? Who can you enlist to help you?

Chapter 21

ARRESTED, CONFINED, BUT STILL EFFECTIVE

Acts 28:30–31; Philippians 1:12–14

The morning bell rang. Mrs. Brooks wrote her question of the day on the white board of her sixth-grade classroom. "What do you want to be when you grow up?"

When Haley read the words, she sprang to her feet. "I want to be an Oscar-winning actress!"

Jenny stood tall. "I want to be on the cover of *Vogue, Cosmo,* and *In Style.*"

Jason zipped to the front of the room, announcing, "Number 22's going to watch his record disappear when I run by."

"Oh yeah? I'm going to make two million blocking you," challenged Mark.

"Don't you two know that the real money's in the Web? I'm going to 'dot-com' it to the top," piped Bethany.

Hollywood hit-makers. New York models. Agile athletes. Business tycoons. Both children and adults aspire to become the latest and the greatest. We forget that, though we celebrate superstars today, their impact on our lives won't stand the test of time. When we near the end of our lives, we're more likely to remember the Mrs. Brookses of the world than the superstars we wanted to emulate. The everyday people who shine their wisdom into our lives will burn brightest in our memories through the decades.

A few ordinary men and women have lived so extraordinarily that their lives light every generation. Among the strongest of these beacons is the apostle Paul. Through his darkest days, he reflected Christ's light to the first-century church.

Today, we still read the letters he wrote while under house arrest in Rome nearly two millennia ago. Even though he was chained to a soldier, he still found a way to write to the Philippians and the Colossians. Let's take a closer look at his letter to the church at Philippi to see how he maintained a positive attitude and an effective ministry even to those who imprisoned him.

A Learned Contentment

From Paul's words, we can tell what occupied his thoughts during the days he was chained to a Roman guard. He mentions his circumstances three times in his short letter, but not in the way we might expect. After affectionately greeting the body of believers, Paul wrote:

> Now I want you to know, brethren, that my circumstances have turned out for the greater progress of the gospel, so that my imprisonment in the cause of Christ has become well known throughout the whole praetorian guard and to everyone else. (Phil. 1:12–13)

What? Paul celebrated his imprisonment? He was content in his miserable circumstances? Later in this letter, he pointed out exactly that.

> I have learned to be content in whatever circumstances I am. I know how to get along with humble means, and I also know how to live in prosperity; in any and every circumstance I have learned the secret of being filled and going hungry, both of having abundance and suffering need. I can do all things through Him who strengthens me. (Phil. 4:11b–13)

Three times Paul emphasized that his contentment did not depend on his circumstances. No conditions, no restrictions, no boundaries affected his contentment. Because Paul drew his satisfaction from the Lord, his disposition didn't drop as his circumstances went downhill. He didn't let the good days distract him or the bad days destroy him; he knew that God was accomplishing His purposes every day.

Paul's outlook allowed God to work through him in incredible ways. It was this common man's uncommon perspective that made him heroic. He relied completely on the Lord. He never cried, "Poor me." He always said, "Use me. Use me in humble and prosperous periods. Use me when food is scarce and when it's abundant." No matter how sour his situation, he never became bitter. Are you cultivating this kind of perspective in your own life?

"But, wait," you might say. "Paul was born a 'glass half full' kind of guy, right?" Wrong. He wrote, "I have *learned* to be content" (v. 11, emphasis added). Contentment didn't come at birth. Paul developed it by taking his eyes off himself and his surroundings and focusing instead on his Savior.

Remember that Paul did not craft his words while sipping pine-apple juice through a straw on some breezy Aegean island. He didn't ponder his points from the top of an Italian peak. He didn't form his ideas in a posh Mediterranean villa. His time in Italy was no Roman holiday. Chained to a stranger in his cold quarters, he penned his joyful message with a shaky hand.

Despite These Chains

Paul had endured many hardships before his arrival in Rome. On his journey from Caesarea to Rome, God's faithfulness carried him through difficult days. Even while stranded on Malta, Paul manifested God's power by surviving a snake bite and healing an elderly man. In addition to hosting Paul and his shipmates, the islanders shared their sand with the crew of an Alexandrian ship. After three months, that ship left Malta with 276 additional passengers (Acts 28:1–11). It sailed to southern Italy and up the coast to Rome, where Paul would spend his house arrest.

Paul "stayed two full years in his own rented quarters and was welcoming all who came to him, preaching the kingdom of God and teaching concerning the Lord Jesus Christ with all openness, unhindered" (vv. 30–31). Paul's hope remained steadfast as the Roman authorities kept him under lock and key and forced him to pay rent for a house near the noisiest part of Rome.

Though most of us have not endured years of confinement, we have all experienced periods when our trials pile one on top of the next. When we find ourselves buried under our pain, we often lose heart. But Paul didn't. Although the Roman authorities could shackle him, they could not restrain his determination to declare the message of Christ.

John Pollock sets the scene:

> No one could leave that hired house untouched, if only to "argue vigorously." It had an atmosphere of happiness with the music and singing which Paul mentions in both the chief letters he wrote from it. His character had not been soured or hardened by troubles. To judge by what he thought important, he was kind, tenderhearted, forgiving, just as Christ had forgiven him. He walked in love, the element

which bound his qualities together. He was still the great encourager, welcoming a man who was weak in faith but refusing to argue about secondary matters. The Romans learned that he lived as he had taught them when he wrote three years before: "We that are strong ought to bear with the failings of the weak, and not to please ourselves. . . . Owe no one anything except to love one another."[1]

Steel and strength. Grace and grit. Both describe Paul's character. Few people on earth in the first century understood the power of God's grace more deeply than Paul. Redeemed from a life of vicious brutality as a rigid, legalistic Pharisee, through Christ's strength Paul became gentle, gracious to the core, understanding, forgiving, and approachable. Though a Jew, he was not only willing to witness to the Gentiles, but also to live among them.

Few have endured more hardship than he withstood as a soldier of Christ. Even more amazing—he never complained about spending over 102 days of his life connected to a man he barely knew. As the days passed, he must have grown very familiar with each of his guards. He ate, slept, and ministered bound to a Roman ball-and-chain. Through his arrest and his lengthy confinement, he never once grumbled. Clearly, he had learned the secret of contentment.

What an amazing attitude! Don't you wish you could respond the same way when you find yourself in a less-than-ideal situation? When you feel like you're under house arrest, you too can live above your circumstances. If a beaten and bruised, falsely accused, wrongly imprisoned, shipwrecked man can do it, so can you. But, like Paul, you must fix your eyes on Christ rather than on your adversity. Though your situation may not change, your perspective will. As problems assail you, tell God about them. Rely on Him to take them away or to give you the strength to endure them. He promises that He will be with you. He guarantees that He will use your trials to increase your trust in Him. When you look to Him, your grumbling will gradually give way to grace.

---

1. John Pollock, *The Apostle: A Life of Paul* (Colorado Springs, Colo.: Cook Communications Ministries, 1985), pp. 286–287.

The Benefits of Looking to Christ in Times of Trouble

Looking to Christ allows us to see beyond the desperation of our situation. Though we still experience pain, we can have faith in the fact that God is accomplishing eternal purposes through our temporal difficulties. "Now faith is the assurance of things hoped for, the conviction of things not seen" (Heb. 11:1). Trusting that God is working His will behind the scenes of our lives allows us to live above our circumstances. And living above our circumstances yields eternal benefits.

First, when we live above our circumstances, *the progress of the Gospel is accelerated.* "I want you to know, brethren, that my circumstances have turned out for the greater progress of the gospel" (Phil. 1:12). The Roman guards took note of Paul's unusual attitude toward his arrest. Through the Spirit of God, Paul's response compelled one guard after another to surrender to Christ. Paul viewed his Roman house as a platform for the Gospel. The soldiers saw his actions as proof of his message. Similarly, when you let Christ's joy supersede your trouble, the Gospel will spread as people ask you to give an account for the hope that you have.

Second, when we live above our circumstances, *the edge of the message of Christ is sharpened.* By Paul's account, his chains had caused the entire palace guard to hear his testimony either from him or from a soldier who repeated his story. Some scholars suggest that 9,000 uniformed men heard the Gospel. The seed of Rome's revival came from one man's message. His enemies' false accusations provided a way for him to get to Rome and spread the truth. In their desire to strangle the growth of the church, they unwittingly caused it to flourish. Remember that God may put you in a difficult place so that you can tell others about Him.

Third, when we live above our circumstances, *the courage of others' faith is strengthened.* As the converted soldiers watched Paul's courage, their boldness increased. They learned from their mentor to proclaim Christ without fear. They discovered that the secret of inner contentment lay in doing "all things through Him who strengthens me" (Phil. 4:13). Christ taught Paul to shine brightly during the dark times by plugging into His power. Just as Paul inspired the soldiers to grow in their belief, you can bolster the faith of those you influence by standing strong in difficult times.

Four Attitudes of a Learned Contentment

From Rome, Paul wrote to the churches at Philippi and Colossae. Both of his letters addressed the secret of inner peace and expressed four attitudes of a learned contentment. These attitudes worked for him under extreme duress. He knew they would work for the Philippians and the Colossians. They will also work for us.

First, *Paul recommended an attitude of unselfish humility.*

> Do nothing from selfishness or empty conceit, but with humility of mind regard one another as more important than yourselves; do not merely look out for your own personal interests, but also for the interests of others. (Phil. 2:3–4)

Remarkably, Paul never used his relationships with the guards for his personal gain. He could have easily asked one of them to appeal to the higher-ups for his release. But he didn't because he knew that God was using his uncomfortable living arrangement to give people a chance to hear about eternal life.

Like Christ, Paul emptied himself and lost the short-lived luxuries of this life in order to win people for the long-term. What about you? Are you willing to sacrifice yourself so that people who oppose you will come to Christ? When you put others before yourself, it draws them first to you and ultimately to Him.

Second, *Paul exhorted believers to have an attitude of joyful acceptance.*

> Do all things without grumbling or disputing; so that you will prove yourselves to be blameless and innocent, children of God above reproach in the midst of a crooked and perverse generation, among whom you appear as lights in the world. (2:14–15)

Paul cut to the chase quickly. He didn't say, "Try to be more positive." He didn't ask, "Who started the fight?" He said, "Don't grumble, and don't ever indulge in petty disputes." Paul knew that the world was watching to see if Christians really treated others with the love of this Christ they worshiped. Paul pleaded for authentic joy because he knew that it would shine a light into a dark-hearted generation. Is your life a light to today's generation? Or do your complaining and arguing cast a shadow on the message of Christ? In a nonbeliever's eyes, your behavior reflects your Savior. Are you representing Him well?

Third, *Paul commanded believers to possess the attitude of strong determination.*

> I press on toward the goal for the prize of the upward call of God in Christ Jesus. Let us therefore, as many as are perfect, have this attitude; and if in anything you have a different attitude, God will reveal that also to you. (3:14–15)

Rather than regretting the road he chose, Paul forged ahead with his eyes fixed on the finish line as he delivered God's message to Rome and beyond. To run the race as Paul did, you must develop undaunted determination.

Fourth, *Paul encouraged believers to pray to God with an attitude of genuine thanksgiving.*

> Devote yourselves to prayer, keeping alert in it with an attitude of thanksgiving; praying at the same time for us as well, that God will open up to us a door for the word, so that we may speak forth the mystery of Christ, for which I have also been imprisoned; that I may make it clear in the way I ought to speak. (Col. 4:2–4)

The seasoned preacher in his sixties knew that the clarity of his message came from the Lord. So, with gratitude to God, Paul exhorted his friends at Colossae to join him in asking for divine direction of his words. Isn't it refreshing to see that he understood that his ability to articulate well was a gift from God? How do you use the abilities God has given you? Do you shine to bring glory to yourself or to point others to Him?[2]

Paul would have never learned contentment without facing pain. The Lord used his difficulties to teach him how to continually rely on Christ. The apostle would have never known the depth of Christ if he had not experienced the pit of despair.

Like Paul, you can grow to be unselfish, joyful, determined, and thankful no matter what circumstances you face. Although your heart probably won't change overnight, the Lord can cultivate these attitudes in you over time. Ask Him to show you how to respond to tough times. He can change your self-focus to Christ-focus, your bitterness to joy, your regret to resolve, and your ingratitude to gratefulness.

2. Reg Grant, "A Star Is Born," *Kindred Spirit* (Winter 2002), p. 11.

✒ *Living Insights*

God has given us Scripture to help us grow. Meditating on specific verses will change our hearts by rooting us in His promises. Let's take some time to look back at the secrets of Paul's peace.

Reread Philippians 2:2–4. Have you put your own interests ahead of another person's needs this week? If so, what will you do to cultivate a humble spirit?

_____

_____

_____

_____

_____

Look again at Philippians 2:14–15. When you want to grumble, what can you do to put a positive perspective on your negative thoughts?

_____

_____

_____

_____

How do a complaining heart and a combative spirit affect other believers? Can nonbelievers see the Gospel in what you do and say? How can you change your attitudes and actions so that your life won't be a hazy reflection of Christ?

_____

_____

_____

_____

Read Philippians 3:14–15. Do you share Paul's determination? How will setting your sights on the eternal prize change the way you react to your next trying situation?

_____

_____

_____

_____

How will the message of Colossians 4:2 change your prayer life? Who can you pray for besides yourself and your loved ones?

_____

_____

_____

_____

 *Questions for Group Discussion*

1. What's the difference between putting others before yourself and letting people walk all over you? How did Christ walk humbly without being a doormat?

2. What's the difference between picking petty fights and pursuing godly confrontation?

3. How do we keep our eyes on the heavenly prize while running the everyday race?

4. How can we tell when the course we're running isn't God's best path for our lives?

5. How can we be thankful for a trial while we're in it?

Chapter 22

SHACKLED, DESERTED, BUT STILL UNDAUNTED

Selections from 2 Timothy

The movie *Saving Private Ryan* opens with rows of crosses arrayed on the shores of Normandy, France. An elderly man hunches over a tombstone. His children and grandchildren shadow him in the background. A tear streams down his wrinkled face as he reminisces about the man who died so he could live.

Set in the days following the greatest battle of World War II, this movie tells the story of a lieutenant and eight men who embarked on a daring mission to find and save the last of four brothers, three of whom had already died in the war. When they finally found the fourth, Private Ryan, the lieutenant was shot while protecting him. With his last few breaths, he grabbed Ryan and whispered, "Earn this. Earn this."

The last words often mean the most. Most of us remember a time when we stood beside Mom, Dad, a grandparent, or a friend, gripped their hand, and heard their final goodbye. Whether the words came quickly or slowly, simple or profound, they are never forgotten.

Perhaps Timothy was at home in Ephesus when Dr. Luke brought another letter from Paul. As Luke recounted Paul's dire situation in a Roman dungeon, the parchment felt heavy in Timothy's hand. As Timothy read the final words of his "spiritual father," he could hear the passion in Paul's pen. "Earn this. Earn this." Paul's words were both simple and profound. For Timothy, they would never be forgotten.

Return to Rome

In the previous chapter we found Paul shackled to a guard under house arrest (A.D. 60–62). Two years later, the Emperor Nero set the apostle free. Unfettered and undeterred, Paul resumed his commitment to preaching the Gospel to the Gentiles. Many believe that with his newfound freedom Paul made his long-sought-after trip to Spain (see Rom. 15:24–28). No one knows for sure. However, we do know Paul took time to mentor his protégés: Titus in

187

Crete and Timothy in Ephesus. He poured his pastoral wisdom into their lives through two letters (Titus and 1 Timothy).

But Paul's liberty lasted only a few years. As Christians grew in number, Nero grew nervous. In an effort to quell this upstart cult, he rounded up its leaders. Paul was snatched at Troas and dragged back to Rome in chains. Instead of being taken to a house, however, Paul landed on the cold stones of the Mamertine Prison.

Down to the Dungeon

Though the site still exists today, few tourists find this dreary dungeon on the list of top ten places to visit in Rome. The pungent odors of sweat and dried blood still cling to the stone walls. The brave ones who descend into the narrow passages find quickly that claustrophobia sidles up to them. Once in the cell, the cold pushes out any memory of the warm Italian sun.

Hans Finzel, in his book *Empowered Leaders*, recalls his visit to the gloomy chamber:

> On an obscure side street a few kilometers from the Vatican, there is a small building thought to house the prison cell where Paul spent his final days. Whether it is actually his prison cell or not is of course debatable. We climbed down into this cramped hole beneath the ground and spent about a half-hour in the dark cell. It was cold, damp, and musty. A small grate in the ceiling allowed a little daylight to shine through. Historians agree that Paul probably lost his life around A.D. 67 when Nero ruled.
>
> As I sat on that cold stone floor, I imagined what it must have been like for Paul in those last days. . . . What a way to spend your final weeks.[1]

From history we know *where* Paul spent the last few days of his life, but from the last verses of 2 Timothy 4, we realize *how he endured* the final weeks before his execution.

Behind Bars

The final verses of chapter 4 give us a peek down through the iron grate above Paul. We can imagine him—a sixty-year-old man,

---

1. Hans Finzel, *Empowered Leaders*, as quoted by Charles R. Swindoll in *Paul: A Man of Grace and Grit* (Nashville, Tenn.: The W Publishing Group, 2002), p. 316.

crippled from past tortures, scarred from beatings, curled up in the dank and dingy cell, working over one final piece that he would later fold quickly and pass into the hands of Dr. Luke, who would then rush it to Timothy.

We can see he's *lonely*:

> Make every effort to come to me soon. (2 Tim. 4:9)

> Only Luke is with me. Pick up Mark and bring him with you, for he is useful to me for service. (v. 11)

> Make every effort to come before winter. (v. 21)

We can see he's been *abandoned* by trusted friends:

> . . . for Demas, having loved this present world, has deserted me and gone to Thessalonica. (v. 10)

> Alexander the coppersmith did me much harm . . . (v. 14)

> At my first defense no one supported me, but all deserted me. (v. 16)

We can see he's shivering with *cold*:

> When you come bring the cloak which I left at Troas . . . (v. 13a)

We can see he's *focused* on God's Word:

> . . . and the books, especially the parchments.[2] (v. 13b)

Paul is emotionally spent. Physically drained. Spiritually famished. But we don't find self-pity. In reading this letter, we can feel his tenderness toward Timothy, but we won't see any bitterness toward God. We can sense the apostle's heart for his friends, but we won't hear any blame. No regrets. As we noted in the previous chapter, Paul lived above his circumstances. Even in facing the circumstance of imminent death, Paul could say:

> I have fought the good fight, I have finished the course, I have kept the faith; in the future there is laid up for me the crown of righteousness . . . (vv. 7–8a)

2. More than likely, the "parchments" included Paul's treasured Old Testament scrolls.

As we near the end of this letter, we realize Paul both knew and accepted his fate. It was time to pass the baton:

> You take over. I'm about to die, my life an offering on God's altar. (2 Tim. 4:6 THE MESSAGE)[3]

Paul, with spare light seeping through iron bars overhead, wrote his last recorded words to Timothy. Shackled and deserted, he stayed at the task of imparting wisdom to his disciple.

Paul's Last Letter—A Survey of 2 Timothy

When we survey the four chapters of 2 Timothy, we discover four sentiments Paul wanted to convey to his trusted friend and protégé. Though written to a young pastor, the book's four themes reveal how all of us can finish this life well.

Chapter One: A Clarion Call to Courageous Living

Timothy and Paul were kindred spirits. More than that, they were family. Paul called Timothy his "beloved son" (2 Tim. 1:2). Though we don't know if Paul had any children, when Paul took Timothy under his wing, he became like a son to him. In these first few paragraphs of the letter, we hear the quivering voice of a father missing his son:

> I thank God, whom I serve with a clear conscience the way my forefathers did, as I constantly remember you in my prayers night and day, longing to see you, even as I recall your tears, so that I may be filled with joy. (vv. 3–4)

Knowing the end was near, Paul was ready to pass the mantle of ministry to young Timothy. Paul exhorted him in four areas. First, he exhorted Timothy to *remember* his heritage (v. 5). Second, he exhorted Timothy to *accept* and boldly act on his calling (vv. 6–7). Third, Paul exhorted Timothy to *suffer* alongside Paul in courageous ministry (vv. 8–12). Finally, Paul exhorted Timothy to *guard* the treasure of faithful principles Paul deposited into Timothy's spiritual account (vv. 13–14).

Before young Timothy could even crinkle the parchment pages,

---

3. Eugene Peterson, *The Message: The Bible in Contemporary Language* (Colorado Springs, Colo.: NavPress, 2002), p. 2172.

he realized he held something more than a letter. It was a blessing. Like Abraham before Isaac, Isaac before Jacob, and Jacob before the twelve sons, Paul blessed Timothy. By now, Timothy was hanging on every word.

Chapter Two: A Checklist for Faithful Service

In the first chapter, Paul put an arm around his son. In the second chapter, Paul spoke like a coach to his star runner before the big meet. He belted out the essentials for running a good race. Soon Timothy would be running apart from his coach, so Paul gave him a checklist of seven lasting commands to tuck in his tunic for the rest of the race:

- Be strong in grace (2:1).

- Be faithful to entrust truth (v. 2).

- Be as brave as a soldier (v. 4).

- Be as disciplined as an athlete (v. 5).

- Be as hardworking as a farmer (v. 6).

- Be as diligent as a workman (v. 15).

- Be as gentle as a servant (vv. 24–25).

In addition to being a great paradigm for ministry, these principles provided a great philosophy of life. Paul needed to entrust Timothy with the essentials to sustain a lifetime of ministry. He knew Timothy's vocation would not be all fun and games. In fact, as Paul noted later in the letter, the Adversary was already setting snares along Timothy's path.

Chapter Three: A Warning List for Difficult Times

In chapter three, Paul moved from coach to prophet. He removed Timothy's rose-colored glasses and gave him a glimpse of reality in ministry. He seemed to say, "Timothy, it won't be any easier for you. In fact, take it from me; it will get worse."

> But realize this, that in the last days difficult times will come. For men will be lovers of self, lovers of money, boastful, arrogant, revilers, disobedient to parents, ungrateful, unholy, unloving, irreconcilable, malicious gossips, without self-control, brutal, haters

of good, treacherous, reckless, conceited, lovers of
pleasure rather than lovers of God, holding to a form
of godliness, although they have denied its power;
Avoid such men as these. (3:1–5)

When rampant apostasy and desperate men sought to under-
mine Timothy's ministry—and Paul knew they would—he exhorted
Timothy to hold fast to what he had been taught (vv. 10–11) and
continue to grow in the Scriptures (v. 14). In a culture darkened
by depravity, Paul gave his spiritual son a compass to guide his
way—the Word of God. He wrote:

All Scripture is inspired by God and profitable for
teaching, for reproof, for correction, for training in
righteousness; so that the man of God may be ade-
quate, equipped for every good work. (vv. 16–17)

Chapter Four: An Urgent Charge to a Ministry of Proclamation

Paul ends the letter as a king knighting his squire:

I solemnly charge you in the presence of God
and of Christ Jesus, who is to judge the living and
the dead, and by His appearing and His kingdom:
preach the word; be ready in season and out of season; reprove, rebuke, exhort, with great patience and
instruction. (4:1–2)

For Paul, the sun was setting on the battles of ministry: the
shipwrecks, the infighting of church members, the beatings, the
turncoat friends, the hours spent laboring over a sermon, the knees
swollen from prayer, the sandals worn out from itinerant preaching,
and the scars from shackles. But for Timothy, the war stories lay
just on the horizon.

Paul realized what was at stake. He knew Timothy would face
temptation to "wing it" through a sermon rather than do the hard
work of preparation, to tickle ears with stories rather than Scripture
(v. 3). He could foresee longtime friends abandoning Timothy. Perhaps even Timothy himself would think, "You know, it's not worth
it." Paul pressed the gravity of Timothy's calling, "I solemnly charge
you in the presence of God . . . preach the word" (vv. 1–2). In
essence, Paul told Timothy, "Ministry is not a choice, my son; it's
a calling, a sacred trust, a charge." It's often the last words that
mean the most. Timothy would never forget them.

Now Paul was ready. For all we know, this letter held the last written words of the seasoned apostle. As he slipped it through the iron grate to Dr. Luke, the battalion of soldiers may have started their march down the planks toward Paul's cell. Each footfall brought Paul closer to his earthly end.

Paul's Earthly End[4]

His death came swiftly—abruptly. Though the exact details of his death remain a mystery, from our knowledge of 2 Timothy and study of Roman executions, the scene comes alive.

Alone and without fear, Paul stared directly into the eyes of the execution squad. Several men held rods with which they would beat him. One held the axe with which he would sever Paul's head from his shoulders. They marched him through the heavy gate and beyond the stone wall that surrounded Rome, past the pyramid of Cestius which still stands today, and onto the Ostian Way, a road bound for the sea. Crowds journeying to Rome would know by the rods and the axe that an execution would soon transpire. They would pass it with a shrug. It happened yesterday, it would happen tomorrow.

The manacled prisoner, walking stiffly, ragged and filthy from the dungeon, did not wince in shame or degradation. The squad of determined soldiers never noticed, as they frowned and stared ahead, that there was a faint smile on their prisoner's face. He was en route to a triumph. The crowning day of his reward. For Paul himself had said, "To live is Christ and to die is gain" (Phil. 1:21). No axe across the back of his neck would rob him of his joy-filled destiny. In fact, it would initiate it!

They marched Paul to the third milestone on the Ostian Way, to a little pinewood in a glade—a glade of the tombs known now as the *Tre Fontane*, where today there stands an abbey in Paul's honor.

He might have been placed overnight in a tiny cell, near the place of his execution. At first light the next dawn, the soldiers took Paul to a stump. The executioner stood ready, stark naked in Roman fashion, axe in his hand. The men stripped Paul and tied him kneeling upright to the low pillar, which exposed his neck. The lictors beat him with rods for the last time. He groaned and bled from his nose and his mouth. Then, without a hint of hesitation,

4. This section taken from Swindoll, *Paul*, pp. 328–29.

the blade gleamed in the morning sun and fell swiftly, hitting with a dull thud the head of the apostle. It rolled down in the dust. In that brutal moment the soul of the great apostle, this man of grace and grit, was immediately set free as his spirit soared into the heavens. Absent from the body, he was at last at home with the Lord.

Closing Prayer

Following Paul from the streets of Tarsus to the Damascus Road to the desert of Arabia to the high seas of the Mediterranean, we've gained invaluable lessons from this unique tentmaker. It's fitting we should reflect on all that God has taught us on this journey. Take some time to remember significant moments along the way when God touched your heart. Then pause in a prayer of gratitude.

> *Thank you, Father, for giving us a life like Paul's, which helps us think deeper, stand alone more confidently, live better, grow taller. Thank you for his courage to the end, his submission to Your plan, brutal though it seems to many. Thank you for his quiet resolve. We look forward to meeting this man and talking with him face-to-face. In the meantime, Father, find us faithful. May we praise You with our lives. May we live for You the rest of our days. We pray in the strong name of Christ our Lord, Amen.*

Living Insights

King Solomon and the apostle Paul started essentially from the same spot. Both had impressive pedigrees. Both were gifted. Both were wise. Both were writers. Both met with God in unique ways. Yet their similarities end at the starting line. They both finished life very differently.

Reread the four chapters in 2 Timothy. Then read the first three chapters in Ecclesiastes.

How did Solomon's philosophy of living compare to Paul's?

_____

_____

_____

How did Solomon's perspective at the end of his life differ from Paul's?

_____

_____

_____

_____

God desires for us to live with eternal glory in mind. However, most of us live as if the end will never come. It's easy to go about our days and live for the moment. Think about your life. Are you living with the end in mind?

_____

Are you heading down the path of Solomon or Paul? One path ends in regret; the other ends in contentment. What is one thing you would change about your life that could send you down the path of Paul?

_____

_____

In the space below, commit to the Lord your desire to finish well. Make a covenant with Him to begin living with eternity in mind.

_____

_____

_____

_____

_____

_____

_____

_____

_____

Questions for Group Discussion

1. Judging from 2 Timothy, one could easily say that Paul finished his life well. What decisions did Paul make during his life that allowed him to finish strong?

2. The last picture of Paul that we have is of him writing this letter to his disciple. It seems at every stage of Paul's life he was pouring himself into people. What principles of discipleship can we take away from the life of Paul? How well are you carrying out Christ's command to disciple others?

3. In reading 2 Timothy, we see a man who was deserted by many trusted friends during his ministry. What are some ways you might handle such disappointment?

4. If you could describe Paul in three words, what would they be?

5. What impacted you the most about the life of Paul? How have you been changed personally by studying his life?

BOOKS FOR PROBING FURTHER

We hope that you've been encouraged as you've accompanied Paul on his journey of faith. Every step of the way, the apostle demonstrated God's unmistakable call on his life. As we've gotten to know him, we've seen firsthand how Paul's courage, passion, vision, and perseverance helped him to reach people for Christ. Not only did he travel well, he finished well, keeping his eyes on the prize.

The following resources will provide wisdom and encouragement for you, no matter where you are on your spiritual journey. They'll offer fresh insights and biblical wisdom that will help you address the issues you face in your everyday life. And they'll also empower you to be more effective in your ministry to others.

Bruce, F. F. *Paul: Apostle of the Heart Set Free*. Grand Rapids, Mich.: William B. Eerdmans Publishing Company, 2000.

Dunn, James D. G. *The Theology of Paul the Apostle*. Grand Rapids, Mich.: William B. Eerdmans Publishing Company, 1997.

Finzel, Hans. *Empowered Leaders*. Nashville, Tenn.: Word Publishing, 1998.

Hawthorne, Gerald F., Ralph P. Martin, and Daniel G. Reid, eds. *Dictionary of Paul and His Letters: A Compendium of Contemporary Biblical Scholarship*. Downers Grove, Ill.: InterVarsity Press, 1993.

Moore, Beth, with Dale McCleskey. *To Live Is Christ: Embracing the Passion of Paul*. Nashville, Tenn.: Broadman & Holman Publishers, 2001.

Pollock, John. *The Apostle: A Life of Paul*. Colorado Springs, Colo.: Cook Communications Ministries, 1985.

Ramsay, William M. *St. Paul: The Traveler and Roman Citizen*. Revised and updated by Mark Wilson, ed. Grand Rapids, Mich.: Kregel Publications, 2001.

Schreiner, Thomas R. *Paul: Apostle of God's Glory in Christ*. Downers Grove, Ill.: InterVarsity Press, 2001.

Stott, John. *The Message of Acts: The Spirit, the Church, and the World*. Downers Grove, Ill.: InterVarsity Press, 1994.

Swindoll, Charles R. *Paul: A Man of Grace and Grit*. Nashville, Tenn.: W Publishing Group, 2002.

Yancey, Philip. *What's So Amazing About Grace?* Grand Rapids, Mich.: Zondervan Publishing House, 1997.

Some of the books listed may be out of print or available only through a library. For those currently available, please contact your local Christian bookstore. Books by Charles R. Swindoll may be obtained through the Insight for Living Resource Center, as well as many books by other authors. Just call the IFL office that serves you.

Insight for Living also has Bible study guides available on many books of the Bible as well as on a variety of topics, Bible characters, and contemporary issues. For more information, see the ordering instructions that follow and contact the office that serves you.

Ordering Information

Paul: A Man of Grace and Grit

If you would like to order additional Bible study guides, purchase the audiocassette series that accompanies this guide, or request our product catalogs, please contact the office that serves you.

United States and International Locations:

Insight for Living
Post Office Box 269000
Plano, TX 75026-9000

1-800-772-8888, 24 hours a day, seven days a week (U.S. contacts)
International constituents may contact the U.S. office through mail queries.

Canada:

Insight for Living Ministries
Post Office Box 2510
Vancouver, BC, Canada V6B 3W7

1-800-663-7639, 24 hours a day, seven days a week
InfoCanada@insight.org

Australia:

Insight for Living, Inc.
20 Albert Street
Blackburn, VIC 3130, Australia

Toll-free 1800 772 888 or (03) 9877-4277, 8:30 A.M. to 5:00 P.M., Monday through Friday
iflaus@insight.org

World Wide Web:
www.insight.org

Bible Study Guide Subscription Program

Bible study guide subscriptions are available. Please call or write the office nearest you to find out how you can receive our Bible study guides on a regular basis.